Half an Inch of Mountains and Rivers

(2016-2025)

[中]何中俊 著
By He Zhongjun

崑崙出版社·纽约
KunLun Press, New York

―當代漢語中堅詩人叢書―

特約編輯： 何中俊
責任編輯： 黑　豐
Contributing Editor:　　He Zhongjun
Responsible Editor:　　Hei Feng

Published by KunLun Press, New York
ISBN:　　978-1-949927-02-3　(Paperback)
　　　　　978-1-949927-03-0　(eBook)

Half an Inch of Mountains and Rivers (2016-2025)
By He Zhongjun

半寸山河　詩歌精選集（2016-2025）
[中]何中俊 著

封面題字： 李君傑
出 版 人： Victoria Zhang

出　　版： 崑崙出版社・紐約
郵　　箱： Kunlunpress@gmail.com
發　　行： 谷歌圖書（電子版）　亞馬遜（紙質版）
版　　次： 2026 年 1 月 第 1 版 第 1 次印刷
定　　價： $35.00

Copyright © 2026 by He Zhongjun, KunLun Press, New York
All Rights Reserved.
No part of this book may be reproduced in any form or by any electronic or mechanical means, including information storage and retrieval systems, without permission in writing from the publisher. The only exception is by a reviewer, who may quote short excerpts in review.

作品內容受國際知識產權公約保護，版權所有，侵權必究

作者簡介

何中俊，詩人，作家，筆名春上樹，秋野珺雪。"每日一詩"詩歌活動發起者，中山市網絡作家協會創始人，2020年華語詩歌實力詩人；民刊《新詩研究》《詩鼎》主編；作品見《詩刊》《星星》詩刊《詩選刊》《作品》《四川詩人》等報刊及海內外主要平臺，入選國內外詩歌多種選本。

主要著作：散文集《路上开放的丁香》，紀實文學《王道》，詩集《在水之湄》《時間的證詞》《劊子手》《春天的草垛》等十六部。

About the Author

He Zhongjun, poet and writer, pen names Chun Shang Shu and Qiu Ye Jun Xue. He is the initiator of the poetry activity "One Poem Per Day," founder of the Zhongshan Network Writers Association, and was recognized as a 2020 Chinese Poetry Powerhouse Poet. He serves as the editor-in-chief of the literary journals *New Poetry Studies* and *Poetry Ding*, and his works have appeared in prestigious literary platforms including *Poetry Magazine*, *Star Poetry Magazine*, *Poetry Selection*, *Works*, *Sichuan Poets*, and other national and international platforms. His poetry has been selected for numerous anthologies in both China and abroad.

Major works include:

> Essays: *Lilacs Blooming on the Road*
> Documentary Literature: *The King's Way*
> Poetry Collections: *On the Banks of the Water*, *Testimonies of Time*, *The Executioner*, *The Haystack of Spring*, and 16 other books.

序

1

据說，在月球上能看到的中國長城，自公元前七八世紀就開始修建，持續不斷地修築了2000多年，總計長達50000多公里，被稱之為"上下兩千多年，縱橫十萬餘裡"。

而乾隆皇帝主持修編的《四庫全書》，前後歷時13年，參與編撰的高官、學者多達360多人，動用了3800多人抄寫。

當年歌德寫他的巨著《浮士德》，前後共花了60年時間，60年，這在古代已經是一個人生命的限度了。

世界文明的奇觀埃及的金字塔，僅胡夫大金字塔占地就達十三英畝，用了兩百三十萬塊石頭，每一塊石頭重約兩噸半。此項建築，據估計費去十萬人工二十年之力。而整個金字塔建築，一共多達七十多座。

五萬余公里的長城，都是人工之力，胼手胝足一磚一石壘上去的；

《四庫全書》是編撰與抄錄人員，一筆一畫來完成的；

巨著《浮士德》，是歌德在房間的角落裡一個字一個摳出來；

金字塔，是數十數百人推動一塊石頭，一寸一寸地砌起來的。

2

這些宏偉的世界奇觀，都是以微末之力，成就曠世之功的。

很早很早的時候，中華文明的始祖黃帝也不過是河南新鄭姬水河一帶一個叫有熊國的部落首領而已，現代來說，也不過是方寸之地。待他統一中國，兼併各個部落的時候，也僅是區區黃河中上游之一角。

夏禹上臺的時候，把他的天下劃分為九個州，"禹收九牧之金，鑄九鼎。"從此奠定了中華古國的基本疆域。再經過秦、漢、唐、宋、明、清，中華人民共和國才有了今天九百多萬平方公里的陸地和數百萬平方公里的海疆。

這片大好的河山，是我中華祖先一代又一代人，一刀一槍從黃沙迷漫的大自然中，從與周圍勢力的戰鬥中搏來的。每一寸土地下，都掩埋著先輩的血汗與骨頭。

滴水成海，聚沙成塔。一個國家如此，一個地方如此，一個人如此，一項事業也是如此。

3

我堅信，每一個人的心裡都有一片自己的山河，有的廣袤，有的博大，有的開闊，有的深幽。

記得有一個著名的作家說過這樣的意思：不要整天想著那些宏大的事物，那些長篇巨著，每天能寫下你的感悟和思考，它的成就和重要絕不遜於那些宏大的篇章。

是的，寫詩多年，越來越覺得這是一場沒有盡頭的馬拉松長跑——一個人終其一生也不過是跑了其中的一小節而已。而每一天，在人來人往，萬物紛繁之中；在一草一木，一言一語之中，我構建著我的藝術山河與詩歌帝國。

我不再拒絕細小，瑣碎和微末。那些主流話語，強勢話語，不僅僅是我關心的內容之一。每天，我都把我新的發現付之於筆端，我沉入自己的大好河山裡。

從最細微之處，也可以開疆辟土，也可以抵達詩歌的殿堂，可以展現廣袤的景場和深遠的時空。

4

人認識世界有兩個方向，一個是橫向的拓展，一個是縱向的深入。

長年累月堅持一件事是一件不容易的。我也不知道明天如何，後天怎樣，這些都不重要。重要的是，我得每天試著走走一兩步，哪怕退了半步也不要緊，下一天又把它補回來。

在馬拉松的長跑中，你不知道你能到達哪裡，能不能抵達終點，但你能做的，就是堅持，不斷地堅持。一分鐘一分鐘地堅持，直到盡頭，或者你在中途倒下！

構建一片自己的山河，是一趟多麼漫長的艱難旅程。然而，在我們有限的生命裡，誰也沒有害怕和退縮。

　　我堅信，再遙遠的征程都是可以抵達的，只是需要我們付出巨大的心智、膽識與勇氣。

　　《半寸山河》，是一個結束，也是一個開始！

　　是為序！

2017 年 3 月初稿，2025 年修訂

PREFACE

1

It is said that the Great Wall of China—visible even from the moon—began to be built as early as the 7th or 8th century BC, and continued for more than two thousand years. Altogether it stretches over 50,000 kilometers, earning the description: "Over two thousand years in time, and over a hundred thousand li in length."

The Siku Quanshu (Complete Library of the Four Treasuries), compiled under the direction of Emperor Qianlong, took thirteen full years. More than 360 high-ranking officials and scholars participated, and over 3,800 copyists were employed.

Goethe spent sixty years writing his monumental Faust. Sixty years—already the span of a lifetime in ancient times.

As for the Egyptian pyramids, those wonders of world civilization: the Great Pyramid of Khufu alone covers thirteen acres and consists of 2.3 million blocks, each weighing about two and a half tons. It is estimated that one hundred thousand laborers worked for twenty years to complete it. Altogether, more than seventy pyramids were built.

The fifty-thousand-kilometer Great Wall was laid brick by brick by human hands, with calloused palms and bleeding fingers.

The Siku Quanshu was completed stroke by stroke by its compilers and copyists.

The monumental Faust was carved out by Goethe, one character at a time, in the corner of his study.

The pyramids were raised inch by inch by dozens, even hundreds, of people pushing a single stone.

2

All these colossal wonders of the world were accomplished through the smallest and humblest of efforts, accumulated over time into feats that astound the ages.

Long, long ago, the Yellow Emperor—the ancestral founder of Chinese civilization—was merely the chieftain of a tribe called Youxiong, in the region of Jishui River near Xinzheng, Henan. In modern terms, it was no more than a patch of land. When he unified China and absorbed neighboring tribes, the territory he controlled was still only one corner of the middle and upper reaches of the Yellow River.

When Yu the Great came to power, he divided his realm into nine provinces and "collected metal from the nine shepherds to cast the Nine Tripods," thus laying the basic territorial framework of ancient China. Through the Qin, Han, Tang, Song, Ming, and Qing dynasties, and finally the People's Republic of China, this land grew into today's more than nine million square kilometers of territory and several million square kilometers of maritime space.

This vast land was carved out by generation after generation of Chinese ancestors—blade by blade, spear by spear—through the swirling sands of nature and through struggles with surrounding powers. Beneath every inch of soil lie the sweat and bones of those who came before.

A drop of water becomes the sea; grains of sand become a tower.

So it is for a nation, a region, a person, and also for any undertaking.

3

I firmly believe that within every person lies a landscape of their own—sometimes expansive, sometimes profound, sometimes wide-open, sometimes deep and secluded.

I remember a famous writer once said something like this: Do not always envision grand things or lengthy masterpieces. If you can record your daily reflections and thoughts, their value and significance are in no way inferior to any grand work.

Indeed, after writing poetry for many years, I increasingly feel that it is an endless marathon—one in which a person, across an entire lifetime, can only run a small segment. Each day, amid the comings and goings of people, the endless clamor of the world; among the grass and the trees, in every word spoken and every movement made, I build my own artistic landscape and poetic kingdom.

I no longer reject the small, the trivial, or the insignificant.

The dominant voices, the voices of power, are merely one category of what I observe. Every day I commit my new discoveries to the page, immersing myself in the vast mountains and rivers within me.

From the smallest of places, one may expand one's territory; one may reach the halls of poetry; one may reveal vast scenes and far-reaching dimensions of time and space.

4

There are two ways human beings come to understand the world: one is by expanding outward, horizontally; the other is by delving inward, vertically.

To persist in one thing over many years is no easy task. I do not know what tomorrow will bring, nor what the day after will be like. None of that matters. What matters is that I try each day to take a step or two forward; even if I retreat half a step, it is fine—I can make it up the next day.

In a marathon, you do not know where you can reach, or whether you can reach the finish line at all. What you can do is persist—minute by minute—until the end, or until you collapse along the way.

To build one's own landscape is a long and arduous journey. Yet within our limited lives, none of us has ever truly feared or retreated.

I firmly believe that no matter how distant the road may be, it is always reachable—so long as we commit our mind, our courage, and our determination.

Half an Inch of Rivers and Mountains is both an ending and a beginning.

This is its preface.

First draft completed in March 2017; revised in 2025

目　錄
Contents

序　I

PREFACE　IV

卷 一
VOLUME I

殘 荷 2
Withered Lotus 3

2016 年春天，致 Robert Bly 4
Spring 2016, to Robert Bly 5

悲憫之湖 6
Lake of Compassion 7

種子是大地的飛鳥 8
Seeds Are the Earth's Birds 9

這些堅硬的部分 10
These Hardened Parts 11

亂石灘之一 12
Rocky Shore I 13

亂石灘之二 14
Rocky Shore II 15

失獨者在病房吞食往事的藥片 16
The Bereft Swallow Pills of the Past in the Hospital Ward 17

匿名者 18
The Anonymous 19

語言的葉子上蛀滿了黑洞 20
The Leaves of Language Are Riddled with Black Holes 21

方式 22
Methods 23

和一株楓樹站在桂山之陽 24
Standing with a Maple Tree on the Sunny Side of Guishan 25

句子 26
Sentences 27

深度意象 28
Deep Imagery 29

北風起時 30
When the North Wind Rises 31

在一朵薔薇裡看見自己的肉身 32
Seeing One's Flesh in a Rose 33

餓狼 34
The Hungry Wolf 35

萬物生 36
All Things Live 37

蹲在時間枝椏上的鳥 38
Birds Perched on the Branches of Time 39

卷二
VOLUME II

黎明這頭火車衝出時光的隧道 42
At Dawn, the Train Bursts Out of the Tunnel of Time 43

影　子 44
Shadows 45

消失的耳朵 46
The Vanishing Ear 47

阿明其人 48
About Amin 49

君　子　國 50
The Gentleman's Nation 51

在　人　間 52
Among Humans 53

一枚柿子的秋天 54
The Autumn of a Persimmon 55

我們這些鳥蛋，孵在這蒼茫的人世 56
We, the Bird Eggs, Hatching in This Vast World 57

所有的安排都是好的 58
All Arrangements Are Good 59

什麼時候開始 60
When Did It Begin 61

当一束光埋进土里 62
When a Ray of Light is Buried in the Earth 63

木頭人的春天 64
The Spring of the Wooden Man 65

故　國 66
The Homeland 67

風　口 68
The Wind's Edge 69

南洋楹頂著一襲月光的袍子 70
The Nanyang Ylang Tree Wearing a Robe of Moonlight 71

春天這個皮匠 72
The Spring Cobbler 73

劍 客 74
The Swordsman 75

悲傷是一場突如其來的雨 76
Sadness is a Sudden Rain 77

我是這樣的一棵樹 78
I Am This Kind of Tree 79

獨 角 獸 80
Unicorn 81

月 光 斬 82
Moonlight Slash 83

卷 三
VOLUME III

在瓦罐上反復地煎 86
Boiling Repeatedly on the Pot 87

一本書就是一朵打開的花 88
A Book is a Flower that Opens 89

我看见动物们都在直立行走 90
I Saw the Animals Walking Upright 91

舀一杯月光 92
Scoop a Cup of Moonlight 93

一頭豬的哲學 94
The Philosophy of a Pig 95

時間簡史 96
A Brief History of Time 97

隱匿的星辰 98
The Hidden Stars 99

大　風　歌 100
Song of the Great Wind 101

新　教　賦 102
The New Song of the Faith 103

明月照大江 104
The Bright Moon Shines on the Great River 105

一場盛大的私奔 106
A Grand Elopement 107

詞語的閃電 108
The Lightning of Words 109

寄身一滴春雨 110
A Drop of Spring Rain 111

高處的事物 112
Things at a Higher Place 113

雙　城　記 114
A Tale of Two Cities 115

一朵雲的心事 116
The Thoughts of a Cloud 117

行　者 118
The Wanderer 119

別樣的安排 120
A Different Arrangement 121

月夜，飛翔的事物 122
Things That Fly Under the Moonlight 123

一封寄往長安的信 124
A Letter Sent to Chang'an 125

卷 四
VOLUME IV

秋天是件蠟染的衣裳 128
Autumn is a Batik Robe 129

以鐵的名義 130
In the Name of Iron 131

大地之書 132
The Book of the Earth 133

在一場虛構裡安眠 134
Sleeping in a Fictional World 135

餵 養 136
Feeding 137

走過那片海 138
Walking Across That Sea 139

西 江 頌 140
Ode to the West River 141

馬塞爾·普魯特斯 142
Marcel Proust 143

2020年的连枷 144
The Flail of 2020 145

潮 水 146
Tides 147

正在行駛的列車 148
The Train in Motion 149

假 苹 婆 150
The Fake Pingpo 151

洗月亮的人 152
The One Who Washes the Moon 153

一 根 鐵 154
A Piece of Iron 155

春 衫 舊 156
Old Spring Shirt 157

捂一個熱詞 158
Keeping a Hot Word 159

失 語 症 160
Aphasia 161

每一塊墓碑就是一座高樓 162
Every Tombstone is a Skyscraper 163

人間往事 164
Human Affairs 165

一隻螞蟻的逃亡 166
The Escape of an Ant 167

卷 五
VOLUME V

木 瓜 樹 170
Papaya Tree 171

秋天，一朵告別的藍 172
Autumn, a Blue of Farewell 173

顫慄的金針花 174
Trembling Golden Needle Flowers 175

刀 客 176
The Swordsman 177

南粵植物志系列之：荔枝 178
The Flora of South Guangdong Series: Lychee 179

南粵植物志系列之：龍眼 180
The Flora of South Guangdong Series: Longan 181

三 棱 鏡 182
Triangular Prism 183

Hawking 184
Hawking 185

內心的懸崖 186
Inner Cliff 187

過 虎 門 188
Crossing Humen 189

平 衡 術 190
The Art of Balance 191

一枚蛋殼的安穩現世 192
The Stable World of an Eggshel 193

平行的世界 194
Parallel Worlds 195

大 鳥 196
The Great Bird 197

河流的一部分 198
A Part of the River 199

殘雪的城堡 200
The Castle of Can Xue 201

小　廟 202
The Small Temple 203

長日將盡 204
The Long Day Is Ending 205

在濕地公園 206
At the Wetland Park 207

摩崖石刻 208
Inscribed on the Cliff 209

卷 六
VOLUME VI

落　草　記 212
Fall into the Grassland: A Record 213

春夜塤事 214
Spring Night's Confessions 215

人間薄事 216
Trivial Matters of the World 217

風　語　者 218
Wind Speaker 219

群山之上 220
Above the Mountains 221

紙上河流 222
Paper Rivers 223

雨夜寫給卡夫卡 224
A Rainy Night Letter to Kafka 225

暮色裡的白鶴是一種隱喻 226
The White Cranes in the Twilight are a Metaphor 227

落在舊巢裡的雨水 228
Rainwater Falling in the Old Nest 229

誰 是 誰 230
Who Is Who 231

藍色妖姬 232
Blue Enchantress 233

尋找博爾赫斯 （組詩） 234
Searching for Borges (A Sequence) 235

空 廟 240
Empty Temple 241

困 境 242
Predicament 243

打開天窗說亮話 244
Opening the Skylight and Speaking Clearly 245

歷史事件 246
Historical Event 247

南方雨季 248
Southern Rainy Season 249

神隱少女 250
The Hidden One 251

看不見的閃電 252
Invisible Lightning 253

大雨，過白衣古寺 （組詩） 254
Heavy Rain, Passing the Ancient White-Robed Temple (A Sequence) 255

卷 七
VOLUME VII

刨 262
Digging 263

困在語言的繭房 264
Trapped in the Cocoon of Language 265

自由的境界 266
The Realm of Freedom 267

山陽道・魏風之阮籍 268
Shanyang Road·Ruan Ji of the Wei Style 269

山陽道・魏風之王戎 270
Shanyang Road·Wang Rong of the Wei Style 271

看不見的世界 272
The Invisible World 273

時間的齒輪 ——寫給 Lee Smolin 274
The Gears of Time —For Lee Smolin 275

涸河 276
The Dry River 277

十面埋伏 278
Ambush from Ten Sides 279

挖藥 280
Digging for Medicine 281

挖地瓜 282
Digging Sweet Potatoes 283

落在寺頂上的雨 284
Rain on the Temple Roof 285

秘密花園 286
Secret Garden 287

秋聲唳鳴 288
Autumn Cry 289

瘦 金 體 290
Slender Gold Script 291

坐在深秋的槐蔭裡 292
Sitting in the Shade of Locust Trees in Late Autumn 293

線 頭 294
Thread End 295

暮靄的思緒 296
Thoughts in the Evening Mist 297

維多利亞灣上空的鷹 298
Eagle Over Victoria Harbour 299

縱 虎 者 300
Releasing the Tiger 301

卷 八
VOLUM VIII

落在阿爾卑斯山的雪 ── 致阿方斯・瓦爾德 304
Snow Falling on the Alps —To Alphonse Walde 305

鑲在藤蔓上的星星 306
Stars Embedded in the Vines 307

布 偶 人 308
The Puppet Man 309

離鄉的麻袋 310
The Sack from the Hometown 311

空中樓閣 312
The Castle in the Air 313

泥菩薩過河 314
The Mud Buddha Crosses the River 315

在黑夜裡相聚 316
Gathering in the Darkness 317

拙　夫 318
The Clumsy Husband 319

慌亂的風 320
The Frantic Wind 321

真　相 322
The Truth 323

被掩埋的巨人 324
The Buried Giant 325

飛　行　術 326
The Art of Flight 327

夜雨打濕的人間 328
The World Wet with Night Rain 329

黃昏裡的哈耶克 330
Hayek in the Dusk 331

別有深意 332
There's More to It 333

隱匿的星辰 334
The Hidden Stars 335

路過的雨如此隱忍 336
The Passing Rain Is So Patient 337

秋後算帳 338
Settling the Account After Autumn 339

蜉蝣生物 340
Ephemeral Creatures 341

杭州媽媽[1] 342
Hangzhou Mom 343

前 夜 344
The Night Before 345

評 論
BOOK REVIEW

在構建與創新中表現思想的深度　　野 松 348
*Expressing Profound Ideology through Construction and Innovation
by Ye Song　355*

卷 一
VOLUME I

殘 荷

肉體漸漸風乾
骨頭靠著骨頭
冰雪裡露出思想的枯枝
孤獨的鷹唱著大風歌

死亡是一截樹樁
靈魂散開，如一捧蓮子
歲月的萼片已經脫落
戰場上還飄蕩著狼煙

蓮蓬斜墜，腐敗的蜂巢
蜉蝣者，湧向西天的黃昏
我是自己的手杖，用最後一根骨頭
把自己的青春埋葬

2016 年 1 月 23 日

Withered Lotus

The flesh slowly dries in the wind,
bone leaning against bone.
From ice and snow, the dead branches of thought emerge.
A solitary eagle sings the Song of the Great Wind.

Death is a severed tree stump.
The soul scatters, like a handful of lotus seeds.
The sepals of time have already fallen away,
yet wolf smoke still drifts above the battlefield.

The seedpod tilts, a rotting honeycomb.
Mayflies surge toward the western dusk.
I am my own cane, using my final bone
to bury my own youth.

      January 23, 2016

2016 年春天，致 Robert Bly

你住在子彈殼的房子裡
用一棵棉花包裹的心
從道德經裡，找到失落已久的
鑽石。你細長的大腳
刀鋒一般，輕輕地跳過
河流和斷崖

棉花外面，是鋼鐵的子彈殼
沒有人能夠看到夜裡的景象
只有孤獨的人，才能和世界為伍
這個時代是此時的，而你
從彼時歸來，躲在雲層的後面

你的頭上是一窩窩青草
手臂比橡樹還長。很多河流
流經你的頭顱，身軀和心臟
內心的事物青草一樣茂密地生長
我看到詩歌的芽尖佔領了天空

Robert Bly，這個春天
我和你抱著一棵走動的樹
在大風裡奔跑吧！

2016 年 2 月 24 日

Spring 2016, to Robert Bly

You live in a house of bullet casings,
with a heart wrapped in cotton.
From the Tao Te Ching you retrieve
a long-lost diamond. Your long, narrow feet,
like blades, lightly leap
over rivers and broken cliffs.

Outside the cotton lies steel—the bullet casing.
No one can see the night's landscape;
only the lonely can keep company with the world.
This age belongs to the present moment,
and you return from another time,
hiding behind the layers of cloud.

On your head, nests of grass.
Your arms longer than oak trees.
Many rivers pass through
your skull, your body, your heart.
Inside you, things grow thick with grass.
I see the bud-tips of poetry seizing the sky.

Robert Bly, this spring,
you and I embrace a walking tree—
let us run into the great wind!

    February 24, 2016

悲憫之湖

劍就懸在頭頂，波浪
不斷地洗刷恥辱。鐮刀
擁著麥浪哭泣。生命的雪線
不斷後退。籬笆繞過村莊
我兩手空空，牽著一頭巨獸
它的影子，讓時光彎曲
我之所愛，一次次煙飛
回射的劍矢，佈滿泥巴的牆垣
誰站在風裡，誰就能窺見
命運的湖底。當恨已成為奢侈
愛的船舶，就會擱淺
湖岸荒涼，月光如刀
割斷拾荒者的目光，鷂鷹飛走
身後，峰壁萬仞
雪豹，從湖水裡露出了頭顱

2016年3月4日

Lake of Compassion

A sword hangs overhead; waves
unceasingly scour away humiliation. A sickle
clutches the wheat and weeps. The snowline of life
keeps retreating. Fences skirt the village.
Empty-handed, I lead a great beast—
its shadow bends time.
What I love, again and again, goes up in smoke.
Rebounding arrows, walls smeared with mud.
Whoever stands in the wind
can glimpse the lakebed of fate. When hatred
has become a luxury,
the vessels of love run aground.
The shore is desolate. Moonlight, like a blade,
severs the scavenger's gaze; the kite hawk flies off.
Behind me, sheer cliff faces in their thousands.
A snow leopard lifts its head from the lake.

    March 4, 2016

種子是大地的飛鳥

我們擁有堅硬的身體
和抵達的渴望。每一個人
都是長著翅膀的飛鳥,內心
有一千隻發芽的手臂,以及
一萬種雨後整齊的聲音

命運是不規則的排列,這古老
的飛鳥。從芨芨草,麥冬
和蒲公英的身體裡,探出
毛簪簪的腦袋和膽怯的目光

我們守著礁石之心,信念的根
四散漂泊,這虛與委蛇的肉身
敲開天空的硬殼。像蒲公英
在大地的子宮裡,緩緩著床

  2016年4月12日

Seeds Are the Earth's Birds

We possess hardened bodies
and the thirst for arrival. Each of us
is a winged bird, inwardly
with a thousand sprouting arms, and
ten thousand orderly sounds after rain.

Fate is an irregular arrangement, this ancient
bird. From the bodies of feather grass, dwarf lilyturf,
and dandelion, it thrusts out
its bristling head and timid gaze.

We keep a heart of reef, the roots of belief
scattered and drifting. This evasive flesh
knocks open the sky's hard shell. Like dandelion,
we slowly implant ourselves in the womb of the earth.

    April 12, 2016

這些堅硬的部分

正如礁石,在海面上
經受一次又一次風雨的洗刷

生活也是潮水,他是柔軟的
不停向居於其中的人發起衝擊

命運的苦酒,浸透了單薄的衣衫
它總想軟化我們缺鈣的骨頭

扒開這些沙石,雜草還有空洞
我們這些堅硬的根系抓緊大地

正如青松之於風暴
正如鐵石之於流沙

沼澤,泥濘,一望無際的黃沙
浮冰下巨大的冰架和陰影

在日常的細屑和碎片裡
我們還剩下最後一付牙齒

2016 年 5 月 20 日

These Hardened Parts

Like reefs, above the sea,
enduring the scour of storm after storm.

Life, too, is a tide—soft in itself,
yet endlessly battering those who dwell within it.

The bitter wine of fate soaks through thin garments;
it always seeks to soften our calcium-starved bones.

Peel back the sand and stones, the weeds and the hollows:
we, these hardened root systems, clutch the earth.

As green pines stand to storms,
as iron and stone stand to shifting sands.

Marshland, mire, endless stretches of yellow desert;
vast ice shelves and shadows beneath the floes.

Amid the crumbs and fragments of the everyday,
we are left with one final set of teeth.

    May 20, 2016

亂石灘之一

我住在石頭上
我在石頭上開出蘭花
世事如棋局,在這
縱橫起落的石陣裡
我也成了被標注的石子

雲朵是棉花的胞妹
石子是骨頭的嫡親
我身體中堅硬的部分
是一場持久的戰爭

長著同一幅面孔
我們不苟言笑。直到
雲朵住上來,蛇蟲住上來
我回到人間,遇到
另一顆流淚的石頭

2016 年 6 月 6 日

Rocky Shore I

I live upon stones.
On stone, I bloom orchids.
The world is a chessboard; here,
among these rising and falling formations of stone,
I, too, have become a marked piece.

Clouds are the sisters of cotton;
pebbles, the closest kin of bone.
The hardened parts within my body
are a war that endures.

Wearing the same face,
we do not speak lightly. Until
clouds move in, snakes and insects move in.
I return to the human world and encounter
another stone, shedding tears.

    June 6, 2016

亂石灘之二

亂石灘的臉越來越小
瘦瘦的,像灘上人
那刀斧削下的輪廓

我吃進了成捆的雜草
腹中的亂雲在飛散
拔開這叢生的植物
才能找到一枚枚鳥蛋

以及數個螞蟻樣褐色的人影
毛細血管都已阻塞
每一條細徑都通向封閉
它們無一例外地雜蕪

還有零星的蔬菜。新式的作物
都留不下種子。飛來的巨獸
坐在留守老人的脖子上

亂石灘,在祖國的葉子上
愈來愈小。像那輪清月
孤懸在桔子樹上

2016年6月7日

Rocky Shore II

The face of the rocky shore grows smaller and smaller,
thin—like the people on the shore,
with outlines hacked by axe and blade.

I have swallowed bundles of weeds;
chaotic clouds scatter within my belly.
Only by clearing this tangled growth
can one find, one by one, the eggs of birds,

and several ant-brown human figures.
Their capillaries are all blocked;
every narrow path leads to enclosure,
without exception overgrown and choked.

There are also scattered vegetables. New kinds of crops
leave no seeds behind. A flying behemoth
comes to sit upon the necks of the elderly left behind.

Rocky shore—on the leaf of the motherland,
growing ever smaller. Like that clear moon,
hanging alone on an orange tree.

    June 7, 2016

失獨者在病房吞食往事的藥片

　　燈光昏暗不明，她的側身
　　像一隻荒原上失群的夜鶯
　　蹲在床頭。四周的靜
　　比水還冷漠。親人
　　都從背景裡漸漸退去
　　這骨髓裡長出來的疼痛
　　無法喊出。護士站
　　只是一個臨時的站台
　　每一個人到站以後
　　只能蘸著夜色的墨汁
　　和著往事的藥片，獨自吞咽
　　那一刻，我看見她的喉結
　　像一個巨大的山洞
　　她是自己脫下的一枚蟬蛻
　　獨自掛在無邊的夜色裡

　　　　2016 年 7 月 20 日

The Bereft Swallow Pills of the Past in the Hospital Ward

The light is dim, indistinct. Her profile
like a nightingale lost on the wasteland,
perches at the bedside. The surrounding stillness
is colder than water. Family
gradually recedes into the background.
This pain, grown from the marrow,
cannot be voiced. The nurse's station
is just a temporary platform;
once each person arrives,
they can only dip the pills of the past
in the ink of night and swallow alone.
At that moment, I see her Adam's apple
like a vast cavern.
She is a cicada shell she herself has shed,
hanging alone
in the boundless night.

    July 20, 2016

匿名者

從飛鳥的肉身取出肋骨
從木柴裡抽出薪火
這人世,飛鳥只有一個靈魂
我們都有一個共同的名字

命名者已經死去千年
後來者只能從經書中找回
我們的任務是:永遠潛伏
在自己人的內部

正如我們修了很多房子
把自己關進去。把惡魔善行
還有美德也分別編號排序
囚于水,囚於火,囚於天地

站在敞亮的地方,說著隱秘的話
匿名者在自己的律令裡
暢行無阻。他不時按下
那遺忘在頭頂的開關

2016年8月19日

The Anonymous

Ribs are taken from the flesh of birds,
fire is drawn from the logs.
In this world, a bird has only one soul;
we all share a common name.

The namer has been dead for a thousand years.
Later generations can only retrieve it
from the sacred texts.
Our task: to remain forever hidden
within our own kind.

Just as we have built many houses,
locking ourselves inside.
Demons, good deeds,
and virtues—each numbered and catalogued,
imprisoned in water, in fire, in heaven and earth.

Standing in the open, speaking secret words,
the anonymous moves freely
within his own decrees.
From time to time, he presses
the switch forgotten overhead.

    August 19, 2016

語言的葉子上蛀滿了黑洞

看起來，是一付多麼堅硬的牙齒
但裡面卻長滿了蛀蟲。不管是
長篇報告，還是精製的短詩
猶其是那廣場上的抑揚頓挫

秋天，是一件華麗的袍子
生命以悲壯的方式，成就
季節毫無節制的欲望。翻開
葉片，你就能找到真相

無懈可擊的辯詞，都能證明
那背後的深謀遠慮。這語言的花粉
鋪滿了大好河山。我們這些潮人
像蜜蜂一樣的蒼蠅，用蜜語

給自己，挖下了無數的黑洞

2016 年 9 月 13 日

The Leaves of Language Are Riddled with Black Holes

They look like a set of hard teeth,
yet inside, they are full of worms.
Whether long reports or finely crafted short poems,
especially the rises and falls of the square.

Autumn is a magnificent robe.
Life, in its tragic grandeur, fulfills
the season's unbridled desires.
Turn over the leaves, and you will find the truth.

Even the most flawless arguments
prove the deep scheming behind them.
The pollen of this language
spreads across the great rivers and mountains.
We, the fashionable ones,
like bees turned flies, with honeyed words,
have dug countless black holes
for ourselves.

September 13, 2016

方　式

木匠滿手血泡
把自己，楔進生活的縫裡
鐵工用彎刀
割斷了生命的臍帶

我是一隻蠶蛹
從黑夜裡探出翅膀
看見秋天，用自己的血
洗去夏天的汗漬

父親的一生，就是彎腰
慢慢地長成一棵莊稼
造機器的張大勇，最後讓自己
成了零件，裝在一部大機器上

2016 年 10 月 18 日

Methods

The carpenter's hands are full of blisters,
wedging himself into the seams of life.
The ironworker, with a curved blade,
cuts through the umbilical cord of existence.

I am a silkworm pupa,
probing wings out of the night,
seeing autumn, washing
summer's sweat away with my own blood.

A father's life is a constant bowing,
slowly growing into a field of crops.
Zhang Dayong, the machine maker, in the end
becomes a single part, installed
in a great machine.

    October 18, 2016

和一株楓樹站在桂山之陽

在桂山，睡著的人還沒翻身
西風，從北邊的崖口
摸過來。在石岐這個地方
你某一天醒來，發現房價
潮水一樣高了。而昨夜西風
也悄悄地摸過了桂山的缺口
房市里的人和西風裡的人
都在哆嗦著

秋楓不識故人
北邊那片城廓連天的平原上
岐江河越來越瘦。車越來越多
只有愛情和鄉愁，還在到處流浪
這塵世的路上，當你和楓樹
牽手，邁進冬天的門檻
你才知道，不管你在山陽
還是盛世，你得到的越來越少
失去的卻越堆越多。這嶺上
每一棵站著的樹，都有一顆
備受煎熬的心

   2016 年 11 月 10 日

Standing with a Maple Tree on the Sunny Side of Guishan

On Guishan, the sleeping have not yet turned over.
The west wind creeps in
from the northern cliff. At this place, Shiqi,
one day you wake to find house prices
rising like tides. And last night, too,
the west wind quietly brushed through Guishan's gap.
People in the housing market, people in the west wind,
shiver alike.

Autumn maples do not recognize old friends.
On the northern plains stretching to the sky,
the Qi River grows thinner. Cars increase.
Only love and homesickness still wander everywhere.
On the roads of this world,
when you hold hands with a maple tree
and step over the threshold of winter,
you realize: whether in Shanyang or in a flourishing age,
what you gain diminishes, what you lose piles up.
On this ridge, every standing tree holds a heart
tortured and weary.

    November 10, 2016

句 子

句子是我用泥巴捏的
冬雨凍僵了它
在立春那天
又被東風吹散了

我是一個鐵匠
從深山掘回它們
七七四十九天
在爐火裡，它們找回了自己的身份

深夜，它酣睡了
這些兒女們，此刻多麼心安理得
我也輕手輕腳，關上門
不讓車聲驚擾

當它們從深藏的岩石裡迸出來時
散成一地的碎玻璃
我含著淚，把它們一一收起
拼接，還原成最初的模樣

2016 年 12 月 23 日

Sentences

I molded sentences from clay.
Winter rain froze them stiff.
On the first day of spring,
the east wind scattered them again.

I am a blacksmith,
digging them back from the deep mountains.
Forty-nine days—seven times seven—
in the furnace, they reclaimed their identities.

Late at night, they sleep soundly.
These children, so content in this moment. I tiptoe,
closing the door,
so the passing cars won't disturb them.

When they burst forth from hidden rocks,
shattering into a floor of broken glass,
I gather them, one by one,
with tears in my eyes, piecing them together
to restore their original form.

    December 23, 2016

深度意象

勃萊深入梅花的內部
感受到讓她們顫慄的風暴
一隻大軍正從海底出發
默溫的祖國，冰藏在
一片葉子的背面

從一個鏡像裡透視另一個鏡像
詩人知道它們連通的關節
他們從一個門裡隱身，又從
另一道門裡逸出

特朗斯特羅姆
把天空鏡片一樣打碎
又重新粘合，光滑如新
鏡子裡全是他古怪的手印

真實的世界
在一隻蝸牛的腳印裡
深度意象的詩人們在海底
看見天空的鳥兒展開了翅膀

2016 年 12 月 26 日

Deep Imagery

Bly delves into the heart of plum blossoms,
feeling the storm that makes them shiver.
An army rises from the seabed;
the silent motherland, frozen,
lies on the underside of a leaf.

Through one mirror, he glimpses another.
The poet knows the joints that connect them.
They vanish through one door,
emerge through another.

Tranströmer
shatters the sky like glass,
then reassembles it, smooth as new.
The mirror bears all his peculiar fingerprints.

The real world
is traced in a snail's footprint.
Poets of deep imagery, beneath the sea,
see birds in the sky unfold their wings.

    December 26, 2016

北風起時

北風從故鄉穿過南嶺
帶著老榆樹的滄桑
帶著日暮蒼山的遼闊
和窮巷野草蔓蔓的世塵煙火
在他淩厲的刀痕裡
走馬燈一樣的過客
日出日落一樣起落在田埂
魚腥草，把自己點燃
二狗的娘，搖醒門外的老瘦竹
這些長身漢，這些不肯苟於塵土
也不肯伏身草叢的人
從岩石裡直起身子
和我站在機器裡多麼相像
那些星子，良心般不肯退場
風裡，多少人放下了前蹄
遊身在這奔騰的河流
我們都是這個時代的獅身人
或者美人魚。北風起時
我為自己找到了活著的證據

2017 年 1 月 9 日

When the North Wind Rises

The north wind passes through the southern ridge of my homeland,
carrying the aged desolation of old elm trees,
the vastness of twilight mountains,
and the worldly smoke of wild grass in poor alleys.
Within its razor-sharp scars,
passersby spin like lanterns;
sunrise and sunset rise and fall along the ridges.
Houttuynia ignites itself.
Ergou's mother shakes awake the old,
thin bamboo outside the door.
These tall men, unwilling to bow to dust
or stoop among the grasses,
rise straight from the rocks,
so much like me standing among machines.
Those stars, like conscience, refuse to depart.
In the wind, many release their forehooves,
wandering through this rushing river.
We are all the sphinxes
or mermaids of this era.
When the north wind rises,
I find proof that I am alive.

January 9, 2017

在一朵薔薇裡看見自己的肉身

黑暗羽毛一樣落下來
火焰的翅膀悄悄收起
黃昏的薔薇躲進樹影裡
像膽小的我，躲避潮水的進襲
她收起來的麻布裙子
有著一兩處撕裂的傷口
多麼羞澀的人，恥於奔走
鮮亮的光芒，紅色的唇
都萎靡成歲月裡的殘跡
抽身而去的事物是走失的馬群
站在明亮月光下的舞者
和那些小販，工人，補鞋者
如花朵，在黑暗裡
悄悄地縫補著，自己的肉身

  2017年2月9日

Seeing One's Flesh in a Rose

Dark feathers fall like night,
the wings of flame quietly folded.
The evening rose hides in the shadows of trees,
like timid me, avoiding the tide's intrusion.
Her folded burlap skirt
bears one or two torn wounds.
What a shy being, ashamed to run—
the vivid light, the red lips,
withered into traces of time.
Things that withdraw are like a lost herd of horses.
Dancers stand beneath the bright moon,
alongside vendors, workers, cobblers—
like flowers, in the dark,
quietly stitching
their own flesh.

    February 9, 2017

餓 狼

不但沒有骨頭
連渣也沒有吐出來
先是李村,接著是張村
連十裡外的七房灣
也被收入囊中

這個專門啃吃良田和石頭的大漢
像個石碾子,它滾過之處
無一倖免。其實它就是一種病
發著高燒,張著億萬隻爪牙
嚼銅吃鐵。它不知道悲憫
是萬物的水滴

它們伏大地上,如你所見
它們總是在等待巧妙的時機
等你打盹的當兒,群起而圍攻
只有歷史躲在鏡子的後面,梳妝
我們,是它殺死的最後一個同謀

2017 年 3 月 23 日

The Hungry Wolf

It has no bones,
not even remnants to spit out.
First, Li Village, then Zhang Village,
even Qifang Bay ten miles away
was swallowed whole.

This giant, specialized in gnawing fertile fields and stone,
like a millstone, leaves nothing unscathed in its path.
In truth, it is a sickness,
feverish, opening billions of claws and fangs,
chewing copper, devouring iron.
It knows not that compassion
is the dew of all things.

They crouch upon the earth, as you can see.
Always waiting for the clever moment—
when you nod off, they surge together in assault.
Only history hides behind the mirror, preening.
We are the last accomplices
it has slain.

    March 23, 2017

萬 物 生

三角梅還掛著小燈籠
人參果一層層疊上去
君子蘭和富貴竹，打開手臂
荔枝樹像個淑女，不溫不火
老榕樹扮著滄桑
辣椒，韭菜和茄子們擠在一堆兒
過著自己的小日子

我就是這流水，這山崗
這叢生的橡樹，霧嵐纏繞在額頭
我的頭上四季分明，或者白雪皚皚
雨水沖涮，平原坦蕩，大河奔流
車馬和牛羊在我的身體裡縱橫四方

我就是這四方穹蓋，這流矢
這星辰，這噴發的溶岩
這地火，這春風，這收起來的劍戈
這懷揣的金戈之聲和拔節之舞
這人世的掙扎，苦痛和大把大把
灑落的水珠和黃金。大地上
遷徙的遺失的奔走的都是我的親人

2017 年 4 月 7 日

All Things Live

Bougainvillea still hangs its little lanterns,
ginseng fruits piled layer upon layer.
Clivia and lucky bamboo stretch their arms open.
The lychee tree, like a gentle lady, neither hot nor cold.
The old banyan wears the guise of time.
Chilies, leeks, and eggplants crowd together,
living out their little lives.

I am this flowing water, these hills,
this clump of oaks, mist winding around my forehead.
On my head, the seasons are distinct,
or snow lies white,
washed by rain, plains broad, rivers rushing.
Carts, horses, oxen, and sheep traverse my body in every direction.

I am this fourfold dome, this flying arrow,
these stars, this erupting lava,
this subterranean fire, this spring wind,
these sheathed swords,
the sounds of golden spears in my grasp, the dancing of shoots.
This world's struggles, pains, and countless
droplets of water and gold scattered across the earth.
On this land, those who migrate, get lost, or run—
they are all my kin.

    April 7, 2017

蹲在時間枝椏上的鳥

它們沉默著,這些消失的森林
毛髮,脫落的皮膚和骨頭
和晚霞一樣隱藏起來的劍光
這些已經長滿了青苔的事物
被水平線抹平的創口
疼痛和細流小溪一樣的悲傷
它們常常在午夜醒來
被折斷的樹枝,被落水的青果
所驚醒。短暫的驚擾之後
是更加深沉的靜默

萬物如謎,雲團在慢慢靠近
它們的翅膀悄無聲息
遠行者露出他石頭一樣的鼻樑
石匠們從石頭裡掙脫出來
他們和樹上的鳥,這即將到來的
欣喜。是多麼慈悲
它把我們從石頭裡救出來
它讓我們從此擁有鐵石心腸

Birds Perched on the Branches of Time

They are silent—these vanished forests:
fur, shed skin, and bones,
and swordlight hidden like the evening glow.
These things, already moss-covered,
the wounds leveled by the horizon,
pain and sorrow like trickling streams.
Often they awaken at midnight,
stirred by broken branches, by green fruits fallen into water.
After the brief disturbance
comes an even deeper silence.

All things are riddles; clouds slowly draw near.
Their wings move without a sound.
The traveler reveals a nose as hard as stone.
Stonemasons break free from the rock.
They, and the birds on the trees,
share the approaching joy.
How compassionate—
it rescues us from the stone,
and grants us from then on hearts of iron and stone.

卷 二

黎明這頭火車沖出時光的隧道

它有十萬隻腳，億萬匹馬力
它有黃金的臉盤，白銀的身子
它有兔毫盞一樣的銀針細線
在它的字典裡，愛情橫掃大江

江流浩蕩，謙卑的門客
放下黑色的簾子。機聲隆隆
清道車開過亂雲堆砌的天空
一千匹駿馬正在萬米的地下嘶鳴

世界如此幽深，狹長
像一座被擠斷的山脈。千鈞鐵騎
從一個火山口，奔向另一個火山口
碎了一地的愛情，找不到悲傷

2017 年 5 月 3 日

At Dawn, the Train Bursts Out of the Tunnel of Time

It has a hundred thousand feet, millions of horsepower.
Its face gleams like gold, its body shines like silver.
Threads as fine as rabbit-hair brushes
run through its dictionary,
where love sweeps across the great river.

The river surges, humble servants
lower the black curtains. The engine roars.
A clearing carriage cuts through skies stacked with turbulent
clouds.
A thousand steeds neigh
deep beneath ten thousand meters of earth.

The world is so profound, so narrow,
like a mountain range snapped in two.
Iron cavalry, weighed in tons,
rushes from one volcanic mouth to another.
Shattered love lies on the ground,
unable to find its sorrow.

    May 3, 2017

影 子

停住的影子，不像我
靜默，神秘，堅定不移
但很快被更多的影子
重疊，交叉或覆蓋

行走的影子，也不像我
迅急，飄忽，驚惶不定
像植物，也像動物
男女不分，陰晴難辨

我們和他們的命運一樣
重疊，交叉，最後被覆蓋

2017 年 5 月 4 日

Shadows

The still shadow is not like me—
silent, mysterious, unwavering.
But soon it is overlapped,
crossed, or covered
by more shadows.

The walking shadow is also not like me—
swift, elusive, anxious.
Like plants, like animals,
genderless, weatherless.

Our fate, like theirs,
overlaps, crosses, and is finally covered.

    May 4, 2017

消失的耳朵

紙屑從紙屑裡穿過
伐木聲敲打著山體
鳥兒集體停止了喊叫
翅膀在翅膀上展開
血液從樹梢流回來

破空之聲,新生或者死亡
頌歌或者哭喊。聲音的墳場
屍體從屍體上誕生
歌聲是一片森林,長出新芽
折斷聲,在鏡子裡碎裂
紋路的長腳,千回百轉

坐在堂上的彌勒,享受著
丟失的快感。他聽見笑聲
骨頭一樣從木頭裡冒出來
一隻貓,當它遠離人世
它就能翻越人類的大山

2017 年 6 月 12 日

The Vanishing Ear

Paper scraps pass through paper scraps.
The sound of logging pounds the mountains.
Birds collectively cease their cries,
wings unfolding atop wings.
Blood flows back from treetops.

A sound pierces the void—birth or death,
hymn or wail. The graveyard of sound
gives rise to corpses upon corpses.
Songs become forests, sprouting new buds.
The sound of breaking shatters in mirrors,
long legs of patterns twisting endlessly.

Maitreya sits in the hall,
relishing the pleasure of loss.
He hears laughter
springing from wood like bones.
A cat—when it leaves the human world—
can leap over mankind's mountains.

    June 12, 2017

阿明其人

他眼睛裡的門關上以後
他身體的每一個細胞都打開了

白天過完了，接著還是白天
阿明走到哪裡，哪裡的燈就打開

黑是最深的白，每一個人都面容皎好
人有般若之心，阿明有觀火之明

從此世界平直了，和人心一樣
拉成了一根長長的直線

生活就在阿明手摸索過的地方起伏
它有了雕刻一樣細膩的紋理

很多年以後，端著一杯老酒
人心是用來聽的。阿明說了一句很老的話

2017 年 7 月 18 日

About Amin

After the doors in his eyes closed,
every cell in his body opened.

Day passed, yet day remained.
Wherever Amin walked, the lights turned on.

Black is the deepest white; every face is luminous.
Humans possess the heart of prajñā; Amin holds the insight of fire.

From then on, the world was straight,
like the human heart, stretched into a long, unbroken line.

Life rose and fell where Amin's hands explored,
bearing textures as delicate as carvings.

Many years later, holding a cup of aged wine,
the human heart is meant to listen.
Amin spoke a very ancient word.

    July 18, 2017

君 子 國

從放大鏡裡
找到崇高的證據
坦蕩的胸懷
裝著這個世界的興衰
每一個人都樂於鹹菜饅頭
讓那些只能鹹菜饅頭的人
恥於行走,博弈
在科學的革命史裡
我們見微知著。在一切
風浪來臨之前,站好隊
在流民的陣營,用
流民的哲學複製他們
在語言的星球站著幾個巨人
但誰都不說話,讓非君子
活得像個白麵饅頭

  2017 年 7 月 20 日

The Gentleman's Nation

Through a magnifying glass,
we find evidence of the sublime.
A broad chest
holds the rise and fall of this world.
Each person is content with salted buns,
making those who know only salted buns
ashamed to walk, to contend.
In the history of scientific revolutions,
we discern the profound from the minute.
Before the storms arrive, we stand in formation.
Among the refugees,
we replicate them with the philosophy of the displaced.
On the planet of language, a few giants stand,
yet no one speaks,
forcing the non-gentlemen
to live like plain, white buns.

    July 20, 2017

在 人 間

我從少年找到老年
那個駝背的女孩扛著一把柴禾
她凍紅的赤足陷在污泥裡
那個犁田的人走過去
他就是一棵移動的艾草
我聞到他身後那苦澀的清芬
那個揚著鐮刀的婦人
差點隨著玉米秸搖斷了她的楊柳腰
那個拉大車的人
那個販賣草帽和領帶的人
那個用土棉紗織出書包的人
那個草叢起身又俯身草叢的人
一個過去了兩個過去了
孩子過去了，老人過去了
男人過去了，女人也過去了
過去了士兵，流浪漢和詩人
天使，就是那一粒麥子
發芽的時候，迎來了黃金時代
拔節的時候，迎來了白銀時代
抽穗的時候，黑鐵時代正在來臨
如今我們都是那些果實，等著
那個將我們采走的人

2017 年 8 月 8 日

Among Humans

From my youth, I reach into old age.
That hunchbacked girl carries a bundle of firewood;
her frost-bitten bare feet sink into the mud.
The man plowing the field passes by—
he is a moving mugwort,
and I smell the bitter, clean fragrance trailing him.
The woman swinging her sickle
almost snaps her willow-like waist along with the corn and oranges.
The man pulling the cart,
the seller of straw hats and ties,
the one weaving schoolbags from cotton yarn,
the figure rising from the grass only to bend back into it—
one passes, then another,
children pass, elders pass,
men pass, women pass,
soldiers, vagrants, and poets pass.
The angel is that single grain of wheat:
when it sprouts, the golden age arrives;
when it stems, the silver age comes;
when it tassels, the era of black iron is dawning.
Now we are all those fruits, waiting
for the one who will harvest us.

August 8, 2017

一枚柿子的秋天

樹葉正在老去
我們站在各自的樹枝上
看著遠山越來越瘦

整整一個山頭,就我一枚柿子
還不肯落下來。你知道
我在等著誰又在盼著誰

秋風用它的利刃
割斷了我們的還鄉之路
蘋果去了城市柚子入了官府

旁邊桔子一家人
草草地摘下燈籠,趕回
淮北那個遙遠的老家

只有我,最後一枚柿子
在秋天的碧空之下,獨自懸掛

  2017 年 9 月 15 日

The Autumn of a Persimmon

The leaves are aging.
We stand on our respective branches,
watching the distant mountains grow thinner.

On the whole hill, I am the only persimmon,
still unwilling to fall.
You know
for whom I wait, and who waits for me.

The autumn wind, with its sharp blade,
cuts off our path home.
Apples went to the city, grapefruit to the officials.

Beside me, the orange family
hastily plucks their lanterns and returns
to the distant old home in northern Huai.

Only I, the last persimmon,
hang alone under the autumn's azure sky.

    September 15, 2017

我們這些鳥蛋，孵在這蒼茫的人世

打魚的人餓了，舀起一瓢江水
就著太陽這張燒餅解饞
城市們群起而來，蠶食著
桑葉一樣連綿的田地
鐵殼蝗蟲，棲息在鄉村這棵大樹上
月光，像塑料一樣被漂白
這江山，這幼子，這村姑
化了眉，描了彩，推上舞臺

風被風趕著，人被人追著
稻子和麥浪，養育著鋼鐵和水泥
股票流行病一樣，迅速傳播
江風浩蕩，幾枚人形樹葉落下來
一些鳥失語，一些鳥正在高呼
一些人，卻像未孵化的鳥蛋
漂流在這蒼茫的人世

  2017 年 10 月 24 日

We, the Bird Eggs, Hatching in This Vast World

The fishermen grow hungry,
scooping a ladle of river water,
satisfying their craving with the sun's flatbread.
Cities gather, swarming,
devouring fields that stretch like mulberry leaves.
Iron-shelled locusts perch
on the great trees of the countryside.
Moonlight, bleached like plastic,
casts over this land, these children, these village girls,
who wear makeup, adorn themselves, and step onto the stage.

Wind drives the wind, people chase people,
rice and wheat waves nourish steel and cement.
The stock market spreads like an epidemic.
The river wind surges, dropping a few human-shaped leaves.
Some birds lose their voices, some cry aloud,
while some people, like unhatched eggs,
drift through this vast, indifferent world.

    October 24, 2017

所有的安排都是好的

在我看來北風的凌亂是好的
能從頭收拾這些舊事物
你忙亂中散開的髮絲是好的
儘管那麼多的負累，你
顧不上這些碎小的細節

夏天的暴雨打折了玉蘭的枝條
我想這也是好的
她從此會更加淡定和從容
和那劫後餘生的人們一樣
抬起頭向著遠方

當你從我身邊離去
我掛念你臉上那硬結的疤痕
我想說，這樣也是好的
我們遵從神的安排，喜樂安好
就像青苗依從於泥土

2017 年 11 月 9 日

All Arrangements Are Good

To me, the disorder of the north wind is good,
able to tidy up these old things from the beginning.
The strands of hair scattered in your hurry are good,
though burdened with so much,
you cannot attend to these tiny details.

The summer storm broke the magnolia's branches;
I think this is good too.
From now on, she will be calmer and more composed,
like those who have survived calamity,
lifting their heads toward the distance.

When you leave my side,
I remember the hardened scar on your face.
I want to say, this is good as well.
We follow the arrangements of the divine, joyful and well,
just as young seedlings obey the soil.

    November 9, 2017

什麼時候開始

我們開始小心地選擇詞語
學會把一些東西咽下去
提防一些事物跑出來
傷害我們最親愛的人
儘管它們常常掙脫韁繩

悲憫不再是一個高處的器皿
順手而及的事情，是在這些
沼澤，岩石，荊棘
和一切尖銳的東西還未出現之前
就將它們妥善安放

我們和命運彼此敵視而又
心照不宣。就像久未謀面的故人
猝然相逢，卻只點頭頷首
而每一次的結束，都是一次
新的出發和抵達

  2017 年 11 月 20 日

When Did It Begin

We began to choose words with care,
learning to swallow certain things,
guarding against some matters
breaking free and hurting those we love most,
though they often struggle against the reins.

Compassion is no longer a vessel on high;
what can be handled with ease
must be properly placed
before the swamps, rocks, thorns,
and all sharp things appear.

Fate and we regard each other with quiet enmity,
yet silently understand.
Like old friends, long unseen,
suddenly meeting, exchanging only nods.
And every ending is a departure,
and an arrival anew.

    November 20, 2017

当一束光埋进土里

甩脫了臂膀。光
從葉子上落下來
碎成了一地黃金
我從天空回到泥土裡
像塊石頭，回到故鄉

當一束光埋進泥土裡
它就是一把低下頭顱的劍
等待那個目光如電的人
光，是一條活著的鞭子
抽痛大地的骨頭

  2017 年 12 月 8 日

When a Ray of Light is Buried in the Earth

Shedding its arms, light
falls from the leaves,
shattering into a field of gold.
I return from the sky to the soil,
like a stone, back to my homeland.

When a ray of light is buried in the earth,
it becomes a sword that bows its head,
waiting for the one with eyes like lightning.
Light is a living whip,
striking the bones of the earth.

    December 8, 2017

木頭人的春天

很多人邁著貓步
用手中的絹扇
拔開亂花飛濺的石頭雨

他被上帝按下了按鈕
他的身體凍結在
一種固體的冰水裡

他成為那只時間的琥珀
活在遙遠的記憶裡
他是一朵只能開放無法收攏的花朵

誰也買不到回程票
當我們從冰河裡拔出腳趾
我聽見木頭人的喊聲破出了冰面

  2018 年 1 月 25 日

The Spring of the Wooden Man

Many people step with cat-like grace,
using their silk fans
to sweep aside the stone rain,
the scattered petals of wildflowers.

He was pressed by God's finger,
his body frozen
in a solid block of ice-water.

He became the amber of time,
living in distant memories.
He is a flower that can only bloom, unable to close itself.

No one can buy a return ticket.
When we pull our toes from the frozen river,
I hear the wooden man's cry break through the ice.

    January 25, 2018

故　國

蕁麻叢裡，蟻族們在奔走
瓦片上的鷂鷹，打著鏇子
我那三千年的新娘啊
還在湖邊，梳著她的長髮

我們在三月，喝著高粱酒
尋找那走失的箭鏃
還有牛羊，山上的親人
在雨水中，瘦下來的江山

故國的人，不種稻粱
也不種刀劍，美人們像山茶花
開在青花碗上。只有連綿的青山
牽著手，站在寒夜裡

故國這枚銅錢，揣在歲月的懷裡
又被月光擦亮

2018 年 1 月 31 日

The Homeland

In the nettle bush, the ants are running,
The hawk on the roof tiles spins in circles.
My bride of three thousand years,
She still sits by the lake, combing her long hair.

In March, we drink sorghum liquor,
Searching for the lost arrowhead,
And the cattle and sheep, the relatives on the mountain,
In the rain, the land grows thinner.

The people of the homeland do not plant rice or grain,
Nor do they plant swords. The beauties, like camellias,
Bloom on blue porcelain bowls. Only the endless green mountains
Hold hands, standing in the cold night.

This copper coin of the homeland,
Clutched in the embrace of time,
Is polished by the moonlight.

    January 31, 2018

風 口

坐在那兒，我抱住
一塊叫時間的石頭
就像抱著，一個睡去的嬰兒
時間久了，我的影子
像一簇櫻花，悄悄地開了
又慢慢地謝了

剛好一束陽光
擋住了熟悉的背影
斑鳩在遠處嘀咕著
好多的事物在我的身上爬來爬去
好多的人，在巷口進進出出

我才坐了一會兒
四周的樹，圍牆，高樓就從我頭上
漫過去。靠在黃桷樹上的時候
我的身體就長出無數的根來
它們要回到大地上，就像我
總是要飛回天空裡

2018年2月24日

The Wind's Edge

Sitting there, I hold
A stone called Time,
As if holding a sleeping child.
Over time, my shadow
Like a cluster of cherry blossoms, quietly blooms,
And slowly fades away.

Just a beam of sunlight
Blocks the familiar silhouette,
The turtledove murmurs in the distance.
Many things crawl up and down my body,
Many people come and go at the alley's mouth.

I have only sat for a while,
And already the trees, the walls, and the tall buildings
Flow over my head. Leaning against the yellow cassia tree,
My body grows countless roots.
They want to return to the earth,
Just as I always want to fly back into the sky.

    February 24, 2018

南洋楹頂著一襲月光的袍子

酒氣慢慢地散了
英雄們握在手心的寂寞
像是一隻只啃食樹皮的蟲子

水妖成群結隊,回到岸上
我站在桃花林裡
是一隻失偶的夜鶯

那麼張惶。這睡去的人世
假裝一切安祥如初
只有流星在尋找

它丟失的光芒
能夠堅守的,都在快速地消亡
只有南洋楹,像個美人

頂著一襲月光的袍子

2018 年 2 月 27 日

The Nanyang Ylang Tree Wearing a Robe of Moonlight

The scent of alcohol slowly fades,
The loneliness that heroes hold in their palms
Is like insects gnawing at the bark of trees.

Water spirits return to the shore in groups,
I stand in the peach blossom grove,
A nightingale, lost without its mate.

So anxious. This world that sleeps
Pretends everything is peaceful, just as before,
Only the falling stars search

For the light they lost.
Those things that can endure are quickly vanishing,
Only the Nanyang Ylang tree, like a beauty,

Wearing a robe of moonlight.

    February 27, 2018

春天這個皮匠

每一種愛和恨
都有著自己的形狀
它們聽從自己的聲音
不斷生長

有時候,它們是一片蘆葦
有時候是條小溪
更多的時候。是青苗
是大樹,是山河,是林海

冬天,我凋裘破敗
走過雪線的人,千瘡百孔
春天這個皮匠,養了許多女兒
杜鵑,木棉,吊蘭,桃李

她們都有一副好手藝
縫合了一切陳舊古老與破敗
還有我內心,那深遠的裂痕

2018 年 3 月 6 日

The Spring Cobbler

Every kind of love and hate
Has its own shape.
They listen to their own voices,
Constantly growing.

Sometimes, they are a patch of reeds,
Sometimes, a small stream.
More often, they are young shoots,
Tall trees, mountains and rivers, forests and seas.

In winter, I wither and fall apart,
Those who have crossed the snowline are full of scars.
Spring, this cobbler, has many daughters,
Azaleas, kapok trees, hanging orchids, peach and plum.

They all have fine skills,
Mending all that is old and worn,
Including the deep cracks within me.

    March 6, 2018

劍 客

他扛著鋤頭,向命運宣戰
扶起弱小的秧苗,豆子
讓土地上的豪強們,那
巨大的闊葉樹,雄偉的山脈
為這些卑微的草木,青苗
和糧食,挪開地方

秋風的劍,從八個方向
進行圍剿。敵人總是躲在
季節的後面。它們出劍如風
它們面不改色,它們略施美人計
在春色的汁液裡,甜美的毒藥
有如甘冽。真正的劍客
是將所有的鋼釘和劍雨
一飲而盡

2018 年 4 月 17 日

The Swordsman

He carries a hoe and declares war on fate,
Lifting the weak seedlings, the beans,
Making way for the mighty rulers of the land—
The towering trees, the grand mountains,
To give space to these humble grasses, young shoots,
And the crops that nourish us.

The sword of the autumn wind,
Strikes from eight directions,
The enemy always hides behind
The seasons. It strikes like the wind,
Unchanging in face, using a subtle beauty,
In the juice of spring's essence,
Sweet poison, as refreshing as a pure spring.
The true swordsman
Drinks in all the steel nails and sword rain,
Without flinching.

    April 17, 2018

悲傷是一場突如其來的雨

上一分鐘，還是陽光萬里
你調侃著那個走失的人
白雲朵朵，是盛開的蓮花
海關的鐘聲，穿過大教堂的穹頂
來回晃蕩。安靜的禮拜寺
淹沒在金色的畫布之上

玉蘭樹輕輕地晃了一下
就像正午趕路的人搖了搖
又一下。路上的人
和天空的雲一樣忙著自己的行程
然後，它猛力擺了兩下身子
一道拉鍊，眨眼之間
就把天空和大地縫合了

我是那棵玉蘭樹
在突如其來的悲傷裡，彎下了腰

  2018 年 5 月 7 日

Sadness is a Sudden Rain

One minute, the sun is shining bright,
You joke about the lost person,
The white clouds bloom like lotus flowers,
The customs bell rings, echoing through the cathedral dome,
Swaying back and forth. The quiet temple
Drowns in the golden canvas above.

The magnolia tree sways gently,
Like a traveler in the midday sun who gives a little shake,
And then another. The people on the road
And the clouds in the sky are busy with their own journeys.
Then, with a sudden force, it shakes twice,
A zipper, in the blink of an eye,
Zips together the sky and the earth.

I am that magnolia tree,
Bowing down in the sudden sadness.

    May 7, 2018

我是這樣的一棵樹

我是這樣的一棵樹
不斷地移植不斷地嫁接
在檔案袋裡，才能尋回
我湮沒已久的姓氏

我也是這樣一種蝸牛
爬過方格磚爬過樹枝
然後站在高高的花壇上
驚異於我那到來的異邦

我看見了一個不同的異鄉
太陽從房頂上升起
月光披上古老的衣裳
鷂鷹從教堂的頂上悄然劃過

我落在我的陰影裡
像一粒藏起奔湧之心的種子
我不知道，我所站立的世界
還是那方小小的陽臺

2018 年 5 月 16 日

I Am This Kind of Tree

I am this kind of tree,
Constantly transplanted, constantly grafted,
In the file folders, only there can I find
The surname I have long forgotten.

I am also this kind of snail,
Crawling over square tiles, crawling over branches,
Then standing on a high flowerbed,
Amazed at the foreign land that has arrived.

I have seen a different foreign place,
The sun rises from the roof,
Moonlight drapes on ancient clothes,
A hawk silently flies past the church's peak.

I fall into my own shadow,
Like a seed hiding a rushing heart,
I do not know if the world I stand in
Is still that small balcony.

    May 16, 2018

獨 角 獸

在假日街,我是一隻
獨角獸。打翻了金髮少女
漂浮在星巴克的白眼

日未央,我剩下的一隻角
抵在銅羅灣的老牆上
旁邊的富貴竹,腆著一張綠臉

踱到滿記甜品店時
我和彈鋼琴的少年
把自己涼成了一杯冷飲

流落於此,和逐水的貝母
有幾分相似。在潮水之上
我慢慢地伸出,開杈的獨角

  2018 年 6 月 28 日

Unicorn

On holiday streets, I am a
Unicorn. I knock over a golden-haired girl,
Floating in the white gaze of Starbucks.

The day is not yet over, and I, left with only one horn,
Rest it against the old wall of Copper Bay.
Beside me, a lucky bamboo flaunts its green face.

When I stroll into the dessert shop,
I, along with the piano-playing boy,
Turn ourselves into a cup of cold drink.

Cast adrift here, I share some resemblance
With the bellflower seeking water. On the tide,
I slowly extend, the branching unicorn's horn.

    June 28, 2018

月 光 斬

群山低伏，他們
把臉側在陰影裡
他們和秋風密謀
林子，用長嘯把星空推遠

朝聖者，正在睡去
這大地的昆蟲
用一根青絲般的繩子
換來一次長久的征程

那些低垂的人
隱匿的青蛙和菌類
被月光塑形，瘦身
成為世間銀色的飛翼

我知道，茅屋的飲者
黃金屋的歌者
都在月光下，磨了一千把刀子
他們伏身，等待著那一刻
啟動一場月光斬

   2018 年 6 月 29 日

Moonlight Slash

The mountains lie low,
Their faces turned in shadows.
They conspire with the autumn wind,
The forest, with a long howl, pushes the starry sky away.

The pilgrims are falling asleep,
The insects of the earth
Use a thread-thin string of green
To exchange for a long journey.

Those who hang low,
Hidden frogs and fungi,
Are shaped by the moonlight, slimmed down,
Becoming the world's silver wings.

I know, the drinkers in the thatched huts,
The singers in the golden mansions,
Under the moonlight, have sharpened a thousand knives.
They bow down, awaiting that moment,
To launch a moonlight slash.

    June 29, 2018

卷 三
VOLUME III

在瓦罐上反復地煎

她把自己分成四季
每天都輪回一次
春天的平和,夏天的暴烈
秋天的冷,冬天的酷
一截病枝,在瓦罐上反復地煎

她把自己分成四份
一份給上帝,一份給醫生
一份給愛人。被蟲蟻
所蛀的那份,自己翻檢,擦拭

不進山,不拜佛
佛是軟心腸,怕他難過
打結的身子,自己解扣
一個人要獨自戰勝一群人

  2018 年 7 月 12 日

Boiling Repeatedly on the Pot

She divides herself into four seasons,
Recycling them every day—
Spring's tranquility, summer's violence,
Autumn's chill, winter's cruelty.
A sick branch, boiling repeatedly on the pot.

She divides herself into four parts:
One for God, one for the doctor,
One for the lover. The part eaten by worms and ants,
She inspects it herself, wiping it clean.

She does not go into the mountains, does not worship Buddha,
Buddha has a soft heart, afraid of his sorrow.
Her tangled body, she untangles herself.
A person must conquer a group alone.

    July 12, 2018

一本書就是一朵打開的花

俯視這十萬大山
我從一條小溪,進入
一條沒有盡頭的長河

沿著這條葉脈
我進入時間的子宮
從一座秘密宮殿走向
另一座宮殿

一千道門次第打開
她從門後出來,遞出
時間的花朵。每一次出場
她都煥然一新

烈士暮年,所有的凋謝
都是合上的書頁
只有愛情,是打開的書
看盡這千年的風雨

A Book is a Flower that Opens

Looking down at these ten thousand mountains,
I enter from a small stream
Into a river that has no end.

Along this vein of a leaf,
I enter the womb of time,
From one secret palace to another.

A thousand doors open in succession,
She emerges from behind the doors,
Handing me
The flowers of time. Each time she appears,
She is renewed.

In the twilight of a martyr's years, all withering
Are the closed pages of a book,
Only love is the open book,
That sees through the thousand years of wind and rain.

我看见动物们都在直立行走

它們等待了很多年
它們蟄伏在山林裡
它們在河水裡念著古老的咒語
就像我每天溫習的古蘭經

大地的引力，比生活沉重
那些晃晃悠悠的頭顱
有著金子般的質地
他們一點一點向大地靠攏
和一株彎下腰的穗子差不多

很多人從石頭裡走出來
他們的血液是白色的水銀
零下一度，我看見雪的世界裡
每一隻動物，都直起了身子

  2018 年 8 月 16 日

I Saw the Animals Walking Upright

They waited for many years,
They slumbered in the mountains and forests,
They muttered ancient incantations in the river,
Like the Quran I study every day.

The earth's gravity is heavier than life,
Those swaying heads
Have the texture of gold,
They inch closer to the earth,
Like a stalk of grain bowing down.

Many people walk out from the stones,
Their blood is white mercury,
At minus one degree, I see in the snowy world,
Every animal stands tall.

    August 16, 2018

舀一杯月光

一個人，擁有一場
奢華的月光派對
正好，用手上的空酒杯
舀起這一杯杯的奶白

第一杯，敬給橫樑山
你養了那麼多的兒女
還有山林和良田
你給了他們靠枕
還交給了他們一副
濁世不阿的骨頭

第二杯敬給岐江河
你用那些魚帆和潮頭
為我們劃出地平線
讓我們在地平線上
找了那副瘦小的翅膀

剩下的這杯
我要在餘下的歲月裡
深一口，淺一口
和你，慢慢地啜飲

2018 年 9 月 18 日

Scoop a Cup of Moonlight

A person, hosting
A luxurious moonlight party,
Just right, with the empty wine glass in hand,
Scooping up this milky cup of moonlight.

The first cup, I raise to Hengliang Mountain,
You've raised so many children,
Along with the mountains, the forests, and fertile fields,
You gave them pillows to rest on,
And entrusted them with bones
That refuse to bow to a corrupt world.

The second cup, I raise to the Qijiang River,
With fish sails and tidal waves,
You drew us the horizon,
So that on the horizon,
We could find those fragile wings.

The rest of this cup,
I'll sip, deep and shallow,
In the remaining years,
Slowly, drinking with you.

    September 18, 2018

一頭豬的哲學

它總是睡著思考
把每一道投向它的目光
和算計，看成是
照耀星空的流螢

磨刀的人，把自己放在刀上
每一天，它打起精神
在遠處雷聲的伴奏下
努力地以一頭豬的立場
活得更像一頭豬

在強盜的邏輯裡
所有的人都是強盜

  2018 年 9 月 20 日

The Philosophy of a Pig

It always sleeps while thinking,
Taking every gaze and calculation cast toward it
As fireflies lighting up the starry sky.

The one who sharpens the knife places himself upon it,
Every day, he gathers his spirit,
Accompanied by the distant rumble of thunder,
Striving, from the position of a pig,
To live even more like a pig.

In the logic of robbers,
Everyone is a robber.

  September 20, 2018

時間簡史

如果氣氛和場景適當
我們可以互為替補
這陶瓷樣的人生
一樣敏感而易碎

我們都是經過時間
淘洗的人。曾經
穿過烈火與暴風雨
流逝的歲月大河奔湧

時間就是那層薄薄的塵垢
猶如新嫁娘的蓋頭
我們都在等待對方
揭開歲月掩蓋的面紗

把悲傷一層層疊起來
把傷痕一道道縫起來
沿著時間的裂痕，你就能找到
那顆奔騰的瓷化之心

2018 年 10 月 10 日

A Brief History of Time

If the atmosphere and setting are right,
We can take turns as substitutes,
This porcelain-like life,
Equally sensitive and fragile.

We are all those who have been washed by time. Once,
We passed through fire and storms,
The river of time, flowing with the years,
Rushing forward.

Time is that thin layer of dust,
Like the veil of a new bride.
We are all waiting for the other
To lift the veil that time has placed upon us.

Layer by layer, we stack our sorrows,
Stitch by stitch, we mend our scars,
Along the cracks in time, you will find
That heart, beating like porcelain.

    October 10, 2018

隱匿的星辰

河流俯身大地
飛鳥潛蹤于楓林
秋天落在群山之上
霜葉紛紛趕路回家

我和這些纖細的草類
風吹雲現，一片蒼茫
大尖山的深處
只有石頭和我愈來愈硬

立在山頭的那只羊
從畫面裡露出了一隻角

2018 年 11 月 13 日

The Hidden Stars

The river bends down to the earth,
Flying birds disappear among the maple trees.
Autumn settles upon the mountains,
Frosted leaves hurriedly make their way home.

I, along with these delicate grasses,
The wind blows, clouds form, all a vast expanse.
In the depths of Dajian Mountain,
Only stones and I grow ever harder.

The sheep standing on the mountaintop
Reveals a single horn from the frame of the picture.

    November 13, 2018

大 風 歌

它要拉出我
身體裡的枝條
像從一棵柳樹的肚子裡
拉出條條綠色絲帶
它不知道,在人間
一夜之間會有多少白頭

有些色澤越來越深
有些人越來越遠
從海嘯到遊絲
就像一個人從伶仃洋
回到石岐河。身上的水印
越來越淺

  2018 年 12 月 18 日

Song of the Great Wind

It pulls out the branches within me,
Like drawing green ribbons from the belly of a willow tree.
It does not know that in this world,
One night can bring so many grey hairs.

Some colors grow deeper,
Some people grow farther away.
From the tsunami to the drifting threads,
Like a person returning from the Lonely Ocean
Back to the Shiqi River. The watermarks on the body
Grow fainter and fainter.

    December 18, 2018

新教賦

麻雀們在天空狂歡
香檳的泡沫河流一樣奔瀉
鷂鷹從大地上撿起
最後一根木棍。青草離離
麗人離離。這人間
都在尋找那些走失的人

馬骨遍地，馬鞭悄悄地歸隱
騎手們正花天酒地
大地倒伏在石頭的洞窟
黃沙們聚集在號令之下
人們頌贊，這馬骨的堅貞
這蝕去的鋼鐵，遙遠的先知

歸來的人群，用肉體去讚美肉體
用馬骨去朝拜馬骨
一塊石頭救出另一塊石頭
一個神靈正從舊路趕來
他要拯救的，是他的替身

2018 年 12 月 27 日

The New Song of the Faith

The sparrows are celebrating wildly in the sky,
Champagne bubbles pour like rivers,
The hawk picks up
The last stick from the earth. The grass is lush,
The beauty is scattered. In this world,
Everyone is searching for those who have gone missing.

Horse bones lie scattered on the ground, the whips quietly retire.
The riders are living it up,
The earth lies prostrate in the cave of stone.
Yellow sands gather under command,
People sing praises of the steadfastness of horse bones,
Of the corroded steel, and the distant prophet.

The returning crowd praises the body with the body,
Worshipping horse bones with horse bones.
One stone saves another stone,
A deity is hurrying along the old road,
The one he is here to save is his own substitute.

    December 27, 2018

明月照大江

肉身是一節鐵軌
鋪在通往群山的渡口
兩岸,一邊
是來處,一邊是歸程
這塵世的寄宿人
一艘小船,一江莎草
風吹草過,時光彎下了腰身

編筐織篦的二爺
是一根扯不斷的經線
走過的人都像河流
唯有二爺,是一條枯溪
明月照大江,枯溪
落滿了荒草和銹蝕的月光

  2019 年 1 月 7 日

The Bright Moon Shines on the Great River

The body is a stretch of railway track,
Laid down at the ferry leading to the mountains.
On both banks, one side is where we come from,
The other, where we return.
This transient world, where we dwell—
A small boat, a river of sedge.
The wind brushes through the grass, and time bends its back.

Old Second Grandpa, who weaves baskets,
Is an unbreakable thread of fate.
Those who pass by are like rivers,
Only Old Second Grandpa is a dried-up stream.
The bright moon shines on the great river,
And the dried-up stream
Is covered with wild grass and rusted moonlight.

    January 7, 2019

一場盛大的私奔

沒人能阻止我
雪,雲層,三千里迷霧
一層層冰淩和岩石
交替奔湧。天空
降下褐色的帷幕
像一襲僧袍。越積越厚
參拜的人點燃自己的手掌

河心傳來的細語
深入每一個張開的血管
千軍萬馬,從地下
從岩石,從樹枝,從骨頭
從窗臺,從溪流,從頭顱
發出了低嘯,奔騰和咆哮

她和風裹在一起,和
鋪天蓋地的雪裹在一起
伸開僵硬的手掌和腳趾
我們被挾裹著踉踉蹌蹌
我,大地,河流,細小的苞芽
都起始於,這場千軍萬馬的私奔

  2019 年 2 月 19 日

A Grand Elopement

No one can stop me—
Snow, clouds, and three thousand miles of fog,
Layers of ice and rocks
Alternating and rushing forward. The sky
Lowers its brown curtain
Like a monk's robe, Growing thicker and thicker,
As the worshippers light their palms in prayer.

The whispers from the river's heart
Penetrate every open vein,
A thousand troops and ten thousand horses,
Rising from beneath,
From the rocks, the branches, the bones,
From the windowsill, the streams, the skulls—
They let out a low howl, a rushing, a roar.

She, wrapped in the wind,
Wrapped in the snow that blankets the world,
Spreads her stiffened palms and toes,
And we, swept along, stagger and stumble.
I, the earth, the river, the tiny buds—
All begin in this grand, tumultuous elopement of a thousand troops and ten thousand horses.

February 19, 2019

詞語的閃電

叢林在顫慄
大地沉睡，黑夜的海水中
青色的魚脊在遊移
隕石劃過，燃燒的森林
多年的遷徙，流浪
一個詞語終於回到故鄉
在邏輯的兩岸，一些人
開始一次漫長的泅渡

我們總是歷史上那個負心人
和逃亡者。被詞語追蹤
足以耗盡，三千里光陰
和數十年的熱忱
只有時間，劃開傷口
剩下的歲月，都是劫後餘生
閃電來臨，所有倒伏的
青草和蕨類，都挺直了腰身

  2019 年 3 月 6 日

The Lightning of Words

The jungle trembles,
The earth sleeps, and in the sea of the night,
The green spines of fish drift.
A meteor streaks across, burning the forest,
Years of migration, of wandering,
And a single word finally returns to its homeland.
On the shores of logic, some people
Begin a long swim.

We are always the heartless ones in history,
And the fugitives,
Tracked by words,
Enough to exhaust three thousand miles of time
And decades of fervor.
Only time cleaves open wounds,
And the remaining years are nothing but survival after catastrophe.
When lightning strikes, all the fallen
Grasses and ferns stand upright.

    March 6, 2019

寄身一滴春雨

內心的火焰,是一首
慢慢涼下來的詩篇
頌詩者,在夜色裡彌散
漁火明滅,披著晨霜的人
像一叢盛開的詞匯

我也要慢一點慢一點
把我內心的涼熱
藏起來。從蓬蒿的髮際
從枯瘦的眉宇,空空的袖管
一路潤過去,到桂山的盡處

所謂的人間,就是一場春遊
從一滴鳥聲開始,春雨一般
落在大地的眉間,我這枚
花骨朵,總是遲遲
無法從一場深眠中,醒來

2019 年 3 月 11 日

A Drop of Spring Rain

The flame within is a poem,
Slowly cooling down.
The poet's voice scatters in the night,
Fishing lights flicker, and those wrapped in morning frost
Resemble a cluster of blooming words.

I, too, must slow down, slower still,
Hiding away the heat and cold of my heart.
From the wild grass at my hairline,
From the thin, withered brows, from empty sleeves,
I will glide on, passing all the way to the edge of Gui Mountain.

What we call the human world is but a spring outing,
Starting with a single bird's song, like spring rain,
Falling gently between the earth's brows. I, this
Flower bud, forever linger,
Unable to awaken from a deep slumber.

    March 11, 2019

高處的事物

太陽是高的
北斗星是高的
它們收割著目光的磁力線

橫樑山是高的
大柏樹是高的
它是另一種頭顱

奶漿菜，斑茅草是高的
鐮刀和蝸牛是高的
新生嬰兒的啼聲是高的

我將它們舉過頭頂

2019 年 4 月 23 日

Things at a Higher Place

The sun is high,
The North Star is high,
They harvest the magnetic lines of our gaze.

Horizontal Ridge is high,
The Great Cedar is high,
It is another kind of head.

Milk thistle and spiny bamboo are high,
Sickle and snail are high,
The cry of a newborn is high.

I raise them above my head.

    April 23, 2019

雙城記

我往返其間,一百斤的肉身
是我的行囊。寄存其間
我像一隻笨鳥,拙於言詞
不尚修飾,疏於場景切換
在消失的城堡,演說者
正在粉刷紅色的宮殿
卡夫卡,艾略特還有石黑一雄
像那些披著長袍的同行者
我們都是城廓的一部分
成為浮土之上,堅硬的支撐
在這宏大的集市
我對自己的分解,樂此不疲
一片尊嚴一斤良心一棵信仰
均可交易出售和暫寄
在此城,先生,我們是屠夫
在彼城,小姐,我輩皆君子

A Tale of Two Cities

I travel back and forth, my hundred-pound body
is my luggage. Storing it here,
I am like a clumsy bird, awkward with words,
not fond of embellishment, unskilled in scene changes.
In the vanished castle, the orator
is painting the red palace.
Kafka, Eliot, and Ishiguro,
like those robed fellow travelers,
we are all part of the city's walls,
becoming solid support on the floating dust.
In this grand marketplace,
I take pleasure in the dissection of myself—
a slice of dignity, a pound of conscience, a tree of faith,
all can be traded, sold, or temporarily stored.
In this city, sir, we are but butchers,
and in that city, madam, we are all gentlemen.

一朵雲的心事

五十年，它從一個小城裡
到另一小城。走了的人
讓它懷念西子洗過的月亮
馬桑樹，刺槐和法國梧桐
這些故舊們，已換了門庭

從西江到湖洲山，大尖山
從和平村到崖口鄉
它的袍子在鼓漲，在消瘦
這個無所適從的人，輾轉在
桂山和岐海的白天和黑夜
獨守在夜晚的眉角，它看見
自己也發出光，成為
銀色月亮的一部分

2019 年 5 月 15 日

The Thoughts of a Cloud

Fifty years, it traveled from one small town to another.
Those who left
Let it remember the moon washed by West Lake's beauty,
the Mayapple, the locust tree, and the French plane tree.
These old things, they have changed their gates.

From the West River to Lake Zhou Mountain, to Dajian Mountain,
from He Ping Village to Yao Kou Township,
its robe is swelling, then shrinking.
This lost person wanders,
between the daylight and night of Gui Mountain and Qi Sea,
standing alone in the corners of the night,
he sees that he too emits light,
becoming a part of the silver moon.

    May 15, 2019

行 者

要努力地咽下去
在一粒稻米或砂子中
還原世界樸素的真相
像一條河吞下群山
和時間撕裂的碎片

自己給自己伐竹，修路
自己割斷自己的頭髮
和念想。和另一個自己
相詰，盤查，對壘直至
談判，妥協甚至握手言歡

還要練習把自己脫下來
或者穿上去。像白玉蘭
穿著雨衣，晨紗或暮色
盈握之間，就是天地吞吐
從自身開始而止於自身

2019 年 6 月 3 日

The Wanderer

You must force it down,
to find the simple truth of the world
in a grain of rice or a speck of sand,
like a river swallowing the mountains
and the fragments torn by time.

You chop bamboo for yourself, build roads,
cut off your own hair,
and your thoughts.
You argue with another you,
interrogate, confront, until
negotiations, compromises, even handshakes.

You must also practice undressing yourself,
or putting it on. Like the magnolia,
wearing a raincoat, morning mist or dusk,
in the space between your hands, the world inhales and exhales,
starting and ending with yourself.

    June 3, 2019

別樣的安排

一隊紅蘿蔔走過來
穿著大紅的袍子
一隊白蘿蔔走過來
把臉別在腋下

巡視官把臉取下來
兩個衛士旗子一樣舉起來
刷刷刷,紅臉白臉大花臉
十裡長街走過臉的方隊
臉的海洋臉的車流

那年我從一片林子經過
看見所有的樹齊刷刷杵在地上
像一排排摘了頭部的將軍
正接受某種徵召的號令

    2019 年 6 月 25 日

A Different Arrangement

A line of red carrots walks by,
dressed in bright red robes.
A line of white carrots follows,
holding their faces tucked under their arms.

The inspector removes his face,
two guards raise their flags like poles,
swish, swish, swish—red face, white face, painted face,
down the ten-mile-long street,
a parade of faces, a sea of faces, a traffic of faces.

That year, I passed through a forest,
and saw all the trees standing stiffly in place,
like rows of generals who had lost their heads,
waiting for some summons or command.

    June 25, 2019

月夜，飛翔的事物

山和樹，是鐵的黑
孤寂，冷傲，活在背景裡
有些人，是金屬的
游走在白和黑的線條裡
夜幕裡，那些結晶的事物
到處閃光，它們
借著銀色的月光重現
各自的光芒。那些
突破重重圍困的心靈
像月光下的鳥，輕盈，柔和
抽離現實的虛影與幻像
我也是一隻銀色的飛翼
借月光重現，一個人的夢境
誠如此刻，你和三尺外的
白玉蘭，合而為一

  2019 年 7 月 17 日

Things That Fly Under the Moonlight

The mountains and trees are iron black,
lonely, aloof, living in the background.
Some people are made of metal,
wandering between the lines of black and white.
In the night, those crystalline things
shine everywhere,
their radiance reborn under the silver moon.
Those souls that break through layers of confinement
are like birds under the moonlight—light, soft,
drawing away from the shadowy illusions of reality.
I, too, am a silver wing,
reborn under the moonlight, a solitary dream.
Indeed, in this moment, you and the white magnolia
three feet away become one.

    July 17, 2019

一封寄往長安的信

再過三十裡就是玉門關了
石頭一樣的黑雲堆在前面
我尋找的唐朝之魂
還不辨蹤跡。此刻的壩上
柳色已青了吧?
渭水的細雨可打濕了你的身子

萬千人,都是一騎輕塵
無力改寫大唐的命運
關前林立的刀兵,晃蕩著
故國的輕愁。我的鞍韉
和我面目一樣有著塵土的色澤

驛更敲過三鼓,長安城裡
也有漏夜之聲。孤獨的人
像簾後的孤燈,在風裡搖
也在雨裡搖。清貧的盛世
卻沒一所草廬,安放
一個人,最清的淺夢

月已隱於山後,驛站的旗角
已漸漸清晰,大漠在前
我去整頓我的瘦馬。遙頌
大安

唐‧開元三年玉門關前

A Letter Sent to Chang'an

In thirty miles, I'll reach the Yumen Pass,
The stone-like black clouds pile ahead,
And the soul of the Tang dynasty I search for
Has yet to reveal itself. At this moment,
Has the willow on the dam turned green?
Has the fine rain of the Wei River soaked your body?
Thousands of people, all are like a light dust
Unable to rewrite the fate of the Tang dynasty.
The swords and spears standing at the pass
Sway with the light sorrow of the homeland.
My saddle, Like my face, carries the color of dust.

The drum of the relay station sounds three times,
And even in Chang'an, the night does not end.
The lonely people, like a solitary lamp behind the curtain,
Sway in the wind, and sway in the rain.
In this impoverished prosperous age,
There isn't even a humble hut
To cradle a person's clearest, shallowest dream.
The moon hides behind the mountain, and the flagpole
At the relay station becomes clearer. The vast desert stretches ahead.
I will tend to my thin horse. From afar, I will praise
Great An.

Tang, 3rd Year of Kaiyuan, In Front of the Yumen Pass

卷四

VOLUME IV

秋天是件蠟染的衣裳

一層層汗漬曬乾
繪成一個人誠實的勞作圖

每一種植物都吸飽了太陽
開出金黃的花來

懷了一個春天
又一個夏天心事的

柿子們桔子們和稻梁們
像出嫁的秋蘭，暈紅了臉

誕下一個幼兒的媳婦
站在原野上，像一株
抖落三千塵埃的千頭菊

在這幅深秋圖上
我淺薄的一生，水落石出
像一塊，大地的眉骨

2019 年 9 月 7 日

Autumn is a Batik Robe

Layer after layer of sweat stains,
Dried in the sun,
Creating a portrait of honest labor.

Each plant drinks deeply of the sun,
Blossoming into golden flowers.

Pregnant with one spring,
And the secrets of another summer's heart.

The persimmons, the oranges, and the rice and millet,
Like autumn orchids on their wedding day,
Their faces blushing red.

A daughter-in-law giving birth to a child,
Standing on the fields, like a chrysanthemum
Shaking off three thousand specks of dust.

In this painting of late autumn,
My shallow life is laid bare,
Like a piece of the earth's brow bone.

    September 7, 2019

以鐵的名義

這個季節裡
我必須以鐵的名義
給自己讓路
像遍山的紅葉
給堅硬的秋風，讓路

山開始露出骨頭
河床也將吐出牙齒
內心的事物
一遍遍淬煉，直到它們
堅如磐石，如精鐵

此後的歲月，沒有囈語
和迎風灑淚
世界用它的硬度
漠視，人生的耐性
和心靈的硬度

原野上，又一個鐵人
為一個莊園，樹起一塊墓碑

2019 年 9 月 23 日

In the Name of Iron

In this season,
I must make way for myself
In the name of iron,
Like the red leaves across the mountains,
Making way for the hard autumn winds.

The mountains begin to reveal their bones,
The riverbed will spit out its teeth,
The things within,
Repeatedly tempered, until they
Are as hard as rock, like forged iron.

In the years to come, no babbling,
No tears thrown into the wind,
The world, with its hardness,
Ignores the endurance of life,
And the hardness of the soul.

On the fields, another iron man
Raises a gravestone for an estate.

    September 23, 2019

大地之書

初秋，過鳳凰山
樹冠基部的一枚葉子
飄落時。譚大爺
從廣元市退了下來

中秋，冠中的葉子
落到我面前
也落在楊二伯的咳咳聲裡
這年輕的礦工
他的矽肺，像一扇
漏氣的風箱

深秋，鳳凰山
飄下它，烏桕樹頂上
最後一片羽毛
山凹的何三娃
鑽出苞谷地，坐上了
開往四川大學的中巴車

2019 年 10 月 6 日

The Book of the Earth

Early autumn, passing through Phoenix Mountain,
A leaf at the base of the tree crown,
When it falls, Grandpa Tan
Retires from Guangyuan City.

Mid-autumn, a leaf from the crown
Falls before me,
Also falls into Uncle Yang's coughing,
This young miner,
His silicosis, like a
Leaking bellows.

Late autumn, Phoenix Mountain
Drops it—on top of the black cypress tree,
The last feather.
In the valley, He Sanwa
Crawls out from the thicket, sits on
A minibus heading to Sichuan University.

    October 6, 2019

在一場虛構裡安眠

孩子，你把大雪看成白色的火焰
它比女人的手掌還仁慈

風是這樣的，進入思想的石窟
一點點驅走殘存的溫暖

每個人都是一塊鐵，互相碰撞
誰先喊疼，誰將敗亡

戴上面具，世界就沒有邪惡和善良
每一塊石頭都笑容可掬

水是特供品，可以澄清可以去污
還可以標注美元和黃金

也可從中找到靈魂的源頭，還原
一片山水的原始與固執

2019 年 10 月 10 日

Sleeping in a Fictional World

Child, you see the heavy snow as white flames,
It is more merciful than a woman's palm.

The wind is like this, entering the cavern of thought,
Gradually driving away the remnants of warmth.

Everyone is a piece of iron, colliding with each other,
The one who cries out in pain will be the one to perish.

Put on the mask, and the world has no evil or goodness,
Every stone smiles sweetly.

Water is a special supply, it can purify and cleanse,
It can also be marked with dollars and gold.

From it, you can find the source of the soul,
Restoring the primitiveness and stubbornness of a landscape.

    October 10, 2019

餵 養

你每天把自己洗一遍
用自己的肉,餵養這個貪嘴的人世
把自己,交給風,交給過往者
最後,你拿著自己的骨頭
你要看著自己,像一根竹子
長出節來,長出雲朵

我也要把自己穿著的這軀殼
剝筍子一樣,一層層
撕掉虛飾,花巧,白紗
然後,把自己交出來
交出來。像那個飼虎者
把自己投入香爐

  2019 年 10 月 19 日

Feeding

Every day, you wash yourself,
Feeding this greedy world with your own flesh,
You give yourself to the wind, to the ones who came before,
In the end, you hold your own bones,
And you watch yourself, like a bamboo,
Growing nodes, growing clouds.

I too, will peel off this shell I wear,
Layer by layer, like peeling bamboo shoots,
Tearing away the falsehood, the trickery, the white veil,
And then, I will offer myself,
Offer myself, like the tiger keeper,
Throwing myself into the incense burner.

    October 19, 2019

走過那片海

北向
我的影子是一條魚
在海水裡越拉越長
拖著的舊時光
像一艘駁殼船,吃水愈深
波浪愈大,愈急
所有的群山
是一群群奔跑的駿馬
在波濤之上,壓過來
急著,把我淺淺印痕
抹去。每一條魚
都在城牆之中
尋找垛口。情侶路為海灘
束上了一條腰帶

2019 年 11 月 18 日

Walking Across That Sea

Northward,
My shadow is a fish,
Stretching longer in the sea,
Dragging old times behind it,
Like a barge, sinking deeper into the water,
The waves grow bigger, faster,
All the mountains,
Are herds of galloping horses,
Pressing down over the waves,
Hastening to erase the faint marks I left.
Every fish,
Searching for its nook
Within the city walls.
The lovers' path, like a beach,
Ties a belt around its waist.

    November 18, 2019

西 江 頌

有的人縶刀子，有的人下釣鉤
一個男人有時候會哭，一條河
它不笑我，像江流般笨拙

一個打魚人，敢於逆水而上
一條河，就敢於亮出自己的肋骨
退潮的河，像餘雙那慢下來的細步

一條寂寞的河，它會喊醒
兩岸的水杉和莊稼。而它睡了
會讓那些失足的亡靈，從此安生

萬物都將逝去，在這個冬天
我和那株異型木棉花，在河邊相遇
她像一條河，打開了自己的花骨朵

在陸泉沙，碰到一群從卓旗山走下來的人
他們身上帶著翠色的風，像一群
在岸邊，移動的樹

2019 年 12 月 2 日

Ode to the West River

Some wield knives, some cast fishing hooks,
A man sometimes weeps, and a river—
It does not laugh at me, clumsy like the flow of the Yangtze.

A fisherman dares to row against the current,
A river dares to show its ribs,
The receding tide moves like Yu Shuang's slow, deliberate steps.

A lonely river calls out,
Waking the water firs and the crops along its banks. When it sleeps,
It allows the lost spirits to rest in peace.

All things will fade in this winter,
I meet the strange kapok flower by the river,
It, like a river, opens its flower bud.

On Luquan Sand, I meet a group of people walking down from Zhuoqi Mountain,
They carry the green winds on their bodies, like a group
Of trees moving along the shore.

  December 2, 2019

馬塞爾·普魯特斯

把蠟燭摁滅
隱身黑暗之繭
時間就是青草的線頭
你不經意地
能抽出一棵樹
一片森林

自己就是那根線
穿山過海。每個隧道
都看不見方向,真相
就在牆面的反射鏡裡
只有倒退的人,才能
從鏡子裡走出來

退一尺,就能進一丈
一個長著無數尾巴的人
一定有十萬隻眼睛
和一千顆心臟

  2019 年 12 月 17 日

Marcel Proust

He snuffs out the candle,
Hiding in the cocoon of darkness.
Time is the thread of grass,
And without thinking,
You pull out a tree,
A forest.

You are that thread,
Passing through mountains and seas. Every tunnel
Has no visible direction. The truth
Lies in the reflection on the wall.
Only those who move backward
Can walk out of the mirror.

Step back one foot, and you can enter ten.
A person with countless tails
Must have ten thousand eyes
And a thousand hearts.

    December 17, 2019

2020年的连枷

連枷落在門檻上。穀粒
麥穗。被雪片掩埋的青草
低頭行走的人，豆莢們
披著厚厚的皂衣，口罩
天黑下來。連枷忙著
翻過自己的門檻
把秕穀，空殼，柴棍和稗子
向更深的黑夜，推

它從中心開始，向四散
放開，如一朵花
一層層傳導它的萼瓣
也正是這黑色的浪
一層層蕩開，一掃這浪尖的
霞光，珠氣和歡場的頌歌

在穀殼翻過來之前
豆子們，翻了一個身，睡下去
獵人，出發了
大地上，立著一根柱子
銘文，讓豆子們讀了一千年

2020年2月2日

The Flail of 2020

The flail falls on the doorstep. The grains,
The wheat heads, buried beneath snowflakes—
The grass, bowed low, the peas,
Dressed in thick, black coats, masks.
As night falls, the flail is busy
Turning over its own threshold,
Pushing the chaff, empty husks, firewood, and weeds
Into the deeper night.

It begins from the center, radiating out,
Like a flower—
Each layer passes through its sepals,
And it is this black wave,
Rippling out, sweeping away the twilight at its crest,
The mist, and the songs of revelry.

Before the husks turn over,
The peas, having flipped over, fall asleep.
The hunter sets out,
And on the earth stands a pillar,
Inscribed, so that the peas may read it
For a thousand years.

  February 2, 2020

潮 水

潮水漲了一寸
竹子紋絲不動,貓頭鷹瞅瞅
又閉上眼。蘿蔔在地下
想挪挪身子,它被釘在硬土裡
潮水又漲了一尺
老黃牛,望了望遠方的天空
它要吃完這片青草
編竹笠的老翁立起身
聽聽,萬物沉寂。只有臘梅
爆開一個花骨朵。院子裡
婚禮如常,盛宴正濃
潮水漲到十丈高時
浪來了,跑出艙的漁夫喊
風卻悄悄地掩上了他的嘴巴

2020 年 2 月 12 日

Tides

The tide rises by an inch,
The bamboo's veins remain still, the owl glances
Then closes its eyes again. The radish, underground,
Wants to shift its body, but it is nailed into the hard earth.
The tide rises by another foot.
The old yellow ox gazes into the faraway sky,
It wants to finish this patch of grass.
The old man making bamboo hats stands up,
Listening to the silence of all things. Only the wintersweet
Bursts open a bud. In the yard,
The wedding continues, the feast in full swing.
When the tide rises ten feet high,
The waves come, and a fisherman runs out of the cabin, shouting,
But the wind quietly covers his mouth.

    February 12, 2020

正在行駛的列車

遠方，我固守著月臺和軌道
鐵軌無止境地撲過來，撲過來

少女在沉思，她倚窗
一幅幅換掉框裡的畫卷

河流奔過來，隧道奔過來
頭髮等白了的四姑娘山，奔過來

輪到大草原，和我擁抱時
維吾爾族大娘，把孩子抱得更緊了

車廂的鉚釘，排成一列省略號
男人的臉女人的臉，依然風塵僕僕

我又立在站台的原點上
像一個新娘，回到她出嫁的地方

2020 年 3 月 7 日

The Train in Motion

In the distance, I stand firm with the platform and tracks,
The railway endlessly rushes forward, rushing toward me.

The young girl is deep in thought, leaning by the window,
Changing the pictures inside the frame, one by one.

The river rushes toward me, the tunnel rushes toward me,
The four-girl mountain, waiting for her hair to turn white, rushes toward me.

When it's the turn of the vast grassland,
The Uyghur woman pulls her child closer in her arms.

The rivets in the carriages line up as an ellipsis,
The faces of men, the faces of women, still weary from the journey.

Once again, I stand at the starting point of the platform,
Like a bride returning to the place where she was married.

March 7, 2020

假苹婆

把自己的手腳
向不同方向扭動。它似乎
努力地向路人，求證
在起灣道上，它
站了十五年。也不喊累

所謂的人間和盛世
就是一棵樹，看不見
另一棵樹。一些人
對另一些人，熟視無睹

站在起灣道上，我手足無措
方向錯亂。多像一棵
怪老頭一樣的假苹婆

  2020 年 3 月 18 日

The Fake Pingpo

Twisting its arms and legs
In different directions. It seems
To strive to seek validation from passersby,
On Qiwan Road, it
Has stood for fifteen years, without complaint.

What we call the human world and the golden age
Is just a tree, unable to see
Another tree. Some people
Are blind to the presence of others.

Standing on Qiwan Road, I am helpless,
Disoriented. Just like
A fake pingpo,
An old, peculiar thing.

    March 18, 2020

洗月亮的人

他又騎著電動車出門了
帶著他的洗刷用品
當然還備著兩個口罩

他說夜班可以多點補貼
疫情期間,他女兒的房子斷供了
前天,女婿告別
說新疆開凍了,鐵路已開工

半夜,我在花園裡被半截詩折磨著
看見他提著清潔桶
扛著清潔用具
正從小區的大門走進來

他身後的月亮又白又亮
肯定被他剛剛擦洗過
我的詩也劃上了句號

    2020 年 4 月 25 日

The One Who Washes the Moon

He rode his electric scooter out again,
Carrying his cleaning supplies,
And, of course, two face masks in hand.

He says the night shift pays more,
During the pandemic, his daughter's mortgage went unpaid,
The day before yesterday, his son-in-law left,
Saying that Xinjiang had thawed and the railways had resumed work.

In the middle of the night, I was tortured by half a poem in the garden,
And saw him, carrying his cleaning bucket,
With his cleaning tools slung over his shoulder,
Walking into the neighborhood gate.

The moon behind him was bright and white,
Definitely just wiped clean by him.
And my poem, too, was brought to an end.

  April 25, 2020

一 根 鐵

一根鐵,在我的身體裡
扭曲,生長
朝不同的方向伸展

後來,它喚醒了更多的鐵
互相攀比,競賽
蓬勃地開出鐵花結出鐵果

它們勾連成林。像一幅畫的
陰影部分

　　　2020 年 4 月 28 日

A Piece of Iron

A piece of iron, inside my body,
Twists and grows,
Stretching in different directions.

Later, it awakens more pieces of iron,
Competing, racing,
Blooming vigorously with iron flowers, bearing iron fruit.

They intertwine to form a forest,
Like the shadowed part of a painting.

    April 28, 2020

春衫舊

門掩了一半,流水漲了一尺
杜鵑叫半聲,喉嚨就被卡住了
就像昨晚暴雨打斷的樹枝
在兩塊石頭之間,橫著

出去的人,悄無聲息
她身後的楊柳,搖了好一陣
我像一把椅子,在庭院裡
放了很久。風陽光和蝴蝶
填滿了這座老宅

桐花萎地,已成泥色
昨夜的歡宴,腳印已沒入青草
此時,她隨桐風而至
會看見,我滿面青苔一身煙雨
我和時間,成了舊人

2020 年 5 月 29 日

Old Spring Shirt

The door is half-closed, the water rises by an inch.
The cuckoo calls once, and its throat is caught,
Like a branch broken by last night's heavy rain,
Lying across two stones.

Those who leave, do so quietly.
Behind them, the willows sway for a while.
I am like a chair, left in the courtyard,
For a long time. The wind, sunlight, and butterflies
Fill this old house.

The tung flowers wither to a muddy color,
Last night's revelry, the footprints vanished into the grass.
At this moment, she arrives with the tung wind,
She will see me, my face full of moss, my body soaked in misty rain.
I, along with time, have become an old friend.

    May 29, 2020

捂一個熱詞

有時候，我像個小母雞
把懷裡的蛋，反復地捂
閒時翻撿一遍，忙時翻撿一遍
有時候，來了個遠客
也拿出來，在燈下照照
接受遠客的驚呼和讚美

有些詞捂久了，會生根
會成為小雞仔，會成為小樹苗
人的一生，和樹一樣
得過刀山，過劍叢，過亂石灘
身體漸漸涼卻。詞越捂越熱
而心卻越捂越軟

2020 年 6 月 5 日

Keeping a Hot Word

Sometimes, I'm like a little hen,
Repeatedly warming the egg in my arms,
Turning it over when idle, again when busy.
When a guest arrives, I show it,
Accepting their praise and astonishment.

Some words, if kept warm long enough, take root.
They grow into chicks, into saplings.
A person's life, like a tree,
Must endure knives, swords, and rocky streams.
The body cools, but the word grows hotter,
And the heart, the more it's warmed, the softer it becomes.

    June 5, 2020

失語症

和牆上那把鐮刀一樣
從土地上離開以後
我開始鏽跡斑斑
我的腰,開始向弧度發展
傾向於聆聽地下的聲音
我的背也開始駝了,重心傾斜

光華之葉掉了一片又一片
如庭前的梧桐
最後,我會脫光寒衣
走在麥田裡
扛著的肉身,是一個問號
重重鐵銹之下,尚能聽到
地下河床,時有深水回聲

2020年6月9日

Aphasia

Like the sickle on the wall,
Once I left the land,
I began to rust,
My waist started to curve,
Leaning toward the sounds of the earth below.
My back bent, my balance shifted.

The golden leaves fell, one by one,
Like the sycamore in the yard.
In the end, I will shed my cold garments,
Walking in the wheat field,
My body, a question mark,
Beneath the weight of rust,
I can still hear
The riverbed below, occasionally echoing with deep waters.

    June 9, 2020

每一塊墓碑就是一座高樓

川北，不入村，謁墓碑
或過山，或入林。碑陣森然
一世祖，二世祖，三世祖
直到最後的一位先賢，順序而列
貧寒或富貴，巍峨或壯觀
或拙笨，或古樸，或簡潔，或繁複
亦如現世，每一個變化的門樓

山高水長，碑文裡
觸摸歷史的凹凸，生命的疼痛
每一個個體無言的悲憤與寒意
和那些永遠沒有說出的梗阻
樸素的巴茅草，正在抽穗
像都市里湧動的面孔和背影
一塊墓碑就是一座高樓
它在人間，比著天地的尺度

  2020 年 6 月 28 日

Every Tombstone is a Skyscraper

In northern Sichuan, not entering the village, I visit the tombstones—
Sometimes crossing mountains, sometimes entering forests.
The rows of stones stand solemn,
Ancestors from one generation to the next,
From the first to the second, to the third, and so on,
Each listed in order,
Whether poor or wealthy, towering or majestic,
Clumsy or ancient, simple or elaborate—
Like the gates of the present world,
Every change of entrance.

Mountains are high, rivers long. In the inscriptions,
I touch the unevenness of history, the pain of life,
Each individual's unsaid anger and chill,
And those blockages that will never be voiced.
The humble grass of the Ba Mao is beginning to flower,
Like the faces and backs in the bustling city,
A tombstone is a skyscraper,
Standing in the world, measuring up to the vastness of heaven and earth.

June 28, 2020

人間往事

一隻螞蟻把另一隻螞蟻打敗
一場風將另一場風
毀屍滅跡

一頭牛從草屋裡出來
殺死自己的心臟
將兩隻角，還給天空

魚群遊過歷史的冰縫
揮著鐮刀的人
又一次被桑麻絆倒

白雪滿懷悲愴
給活著的人蓋上被角
蒙上眼睛，我看見
死去多年的狼，騰空而起

    2020 年 9 月 18 日

Human Affairs

An ant defeats another ant.
A gust of wind wipes out another gust,
leaving no trace.

A cow steps out of the thatched hut,
kills its own heart,
and returns its horns to the sky.

A school of fish swims through the ice cracks of history,
and the one who wields the sickle
is tripped once more by the mulberry and hemp.

Snow falls, heavy with sorrow,
covering the living with a blanket,
blinding their eyes. I see
wolves, long dead, rise into the air.

    September 18, 2020

一隻螞蟻的逃亡

偌大的江湖，沒有菊花和刀
看不見一隻草垛
我在缸沿上走了一百個來回

只有風，從樹縫漏過來
給了我一付輕盈的翅膀
作為螞蟻，我坐擁了一座米的江山

烈重的米香，淹沒了我的唾液
我的願望，是和一粒雪
相擁一生。我不知道

一粒米的手，牽著十萬座山脈
我開始挖山，塌一座我挖走一座
我開始分不清，山與餓哪個更重

我的命運在於：推開大米，找到出路
而大米的命運：堵住漏洞，平息戰爭
結局是：我在缸裡變身米粒
只是色黑，且略顯骨硬

　　2020 年 9 月 22 日

The Escape of an Ant

In this vast world, there are no chrysanthemums or knives,
No haystacks to be seen.
I walked a hundred times around the edge of the jar.

Only the wind, slipping through the cracks in the trees,
Gave me a pair of light wings.
As an ant, I ruled over a kingdom of rice.

The heavy fragrance of rice drowned my saliva,
My wish was to embrace a grain of snow for a lifetime.
But I didn't know...

The hand of a single grain of rice holds ten thousand mountains.
I began to dig mountains;
When one collapsed, I dug another.

I began to lose track— which was heavier, the mountains or hunger?
My fate lies in: pushing aside the rice, finding a way out.
And the fate of the rice: blocking the gaps, quelling the war.
The conclusion is: I transform into a grain of rice in the jar,
Only black in color, with slightly harder bones.

    September 22, 2020

卷 五
VOLUME V

木 瓜 樹

它就是個老婦人
每一滴眼淚長大了
就是一棵木瓜
她不斷地流淚流淚流淚
而那些過路的人
談情說愛的人
不斷地索取她淚的果實

如你所見，如今
她乳房乾癟，四肢低垂
只剩下乾瘦的軀幹
淚幹了，萬千子孫無蹤跡
她還在拼命地擠，擠
一滴乳白色的液體
掛在她石頭般的皮膚上

   2020 年 10 月 14 日

Papaya Tree

It's like an old woman,
Each drop of her tears has grown
Into a papaya.
She keeps crying, crying, crying,
And those passing by,
Those in love,
Keep taking the fruit of her tears.

As you can see, now,
Her breasts are shriveled, her limbs droop,
Only a thin, dry trunk remains.
Her tears have dried, and her countless descendants have vanished.
Yet still, she struggles, squeezing, squeezing,
A drop of milky liquid
Hangs from her stone-like skin.

    October 14, 2020

秋天，一朵告別的藍

翅膀離天空，越來越近
離大地就越來越遠
我抱緊你，是因為我將離開
就像葉子掉落前，抱緊樹幹
而我的離開，是因為
一隻鳥對另一隻鳥的深戀

我紅色的愛人，她把自己
一點點交還給河流和大地
像一個人，從肉體中抽身而去
山路又遠又硬，狐兔們也少來問津
老牛累得像一塊石頭
割草的少女，也日漸枯黃

只有藍是我自己的，空曠且輕盈
從簷角開始，挽住人間的炊煙
和傷痛。掩蓋那些雨後醃髒的漬跡
最後，我把我交還給你
就像你，交出了另一個自己

2020 年 11 月 8 日

Autumn, a Blue of Farewell

Wings move closer to the sky,
And further from the earth.
I hold you tight, because I will leave,
Like a leaf clinging to the tree before it falls.
And my leaving is because
One bird deeply loves another.

My red lover, she slowly
Gives herself back to the river and the earth,
Like someone pulling away from their body.
The mountain paths are long and hard,
Foxes and rabbits seldom visit,
The old ox is as weary as a stone,
The girl cutting grass grows more yellow each day.

Only blue is mine, vast and light,
From the eaves it reaches, holding the world's smoke
And its pain. It covers the stains
Of rain-soaked dirt.
At last, I give myself back to you,
Just as you gave up another version of yourself.

    November 8, 2020

顫慄的金針花

那一刻，我不知道有多少
雷聲在遠處炸響
有多少風
正聚集著暴發的力量
還有多少眼睛，在暗處
把它們的針芒射向你的花蕊

黑夜開始向我發起圍攻
我和你一樣，冷從足踝開始
恐懼水一樣從頭上澆下來
未知的事物從遠處向我們逼近
振動是從髮絲的末梢開始的
沿著神經線，它們傳遞著

沒人知道開始
驚恐的表情風一樣展開
你搖著自己，也搖著我
瘦弱的枝葉。我舉起的金針
再一次，把自己刺傷

  2020 年 11 月 10 日

Trembling Golden Needle Flowers

At that moment, I did not know how many
Thunderclaps were exploding in the distance,
How many winds
Were gathering their force to burst,
And how many eyes, in the dark,
Were aiming their sharp needles at your petals.

The night began to launch its siege on me.
Like you, coldness started from my ankles,
Fear, like water, poured down from my head.
Unknown things approached us from afar.
The vibrations started at the tips of my hair,
Spreading along my nerves, they carried on.

No one knows where it began.
Expressions of panic unfurled like the wind.
You shook yourself, and you shook me—
The fragile branches and leaves. I raised the golden needles
Once again, wounding myself.

    November 10, 2020

刀 客

禦風,禦人,禦丘壑
我的另一個身份是刀客
水波未起,我已身中數刀
更多的時候,我就是那把刀
瞬息之間和寒光同時出擊
空氣凝固,很久,很久
該發生的事還是沒有發生

刀客的上乘境界,就是
周身無刀而周身是刀
不帶刀,卻鋒利過人
我所練成的絕技是:樹一樣
中一刀,高一寸
多年以後。作為一名刀客
我收起了最後一縷鋒芒

  2020 年 12 月 16 日

The Swordsman

Defying wind, defying men, defying hills and valleys,
My other identity is that of a swordsman.
Before the water stirs, I am already pierced by several blades.
More often than not, I am the blade itself,
Striking in an instant, together with the cold gleam of steel.
The air stiffens, for a long, long time.
What was meant to happen still hasn't.

The highest realm of a swordsman is to
Have no sword at all, yet be a sword through and through.
Without carrying a blade, yet sharper than any man.
The ultimate skill I have mastered is this: Like a tree,
When struck by a blade, it grows an inch taller.
Years later, as a swordsman,
I put away my last edge of sharpness.

    December 16, 2020

南粵植物志系列之：荔枝

南粵廣嶼，他們都是親兄弟
天尚平權，蔑視一人獨大
每一棵樹自由伸展。一樣具備
華美的雍容之姿
手牽手，就能計量一個村莊
一個島嶼，一片沙洲，一群人
一個時代能夠抵達的寬廣與縱深

在所有的堤畔，他們排成古老的隊列
在一切群集，獨居之處紮根
成為每一個村落的陣容
風過洋面，雨如劍陣，拿著電鋸的雷神
敲響銅盆咆哮，浩大的荔枝家族
從未露出被攻擊的破綻

那一年，香山縣的荔枝們拒絕開花
那一年，三千個壯漢共赴南洋

2020 年 12 月 18 日

The Flora of South Guangdong Series: Lychee

In the vast islands of South Guangdong, they are all brothers,
When heaven still holds equality, no one is greater than the rest.
Every tree stretches freely, each adorned
With the graceful dignity of beauty.
Hand in hand, they can measure a village,
An island, a sandbar, a group of people,
The vastness and depth of an era they can reach.

On every embankment, they form ancient lines,
In every gathering and solitary place, they take root,
Becoming the formation of each village.
The wind sweeps over the ocean, the rain falls like a blade array,
With Thor wielding a chainsaw,
Striking the copper basin with a roar,
The mighty Lychee family
Has never shown a weakness under attack.

That year, the lychees of Xiangshan County refused to bloom,
That year, three thousand strong men set sail for Nanyang.

December 18, 2020

南粵植物志系列之：龍眼

金戈之聲漸漸遠去
懷璧的人，聽見長空一聲雁鳴
抬望眼，看不見宮牆的簷角
一顆碩大的淚珠，濺起塵埃

此後，姓氏成為遙遠的記痕
他們開始散落民間，融入尋常巷陌
向更深，更遠，更幽的角落伸出觸角
在河堤，湖岸，台壩，簷角

那來自骨子裡的悲痛，在人間
不可抬頭，把姿態低下去，再低下去
可是，他們忘了，真正的貴族精神
是無法掩藏的。當你打開
白玉般的果肉之門，那生命之核

2020 年 12 月 18 日

The Flora of South Guangdong Series: Longan

The sound of battle gradually fades away,
The one who holds treasure hears a lone goose call in the vast sky,
Raising their gaze, they can no longer see the eaves of the palace walls,
A single large teardrop splashes, stirring the dust.

From then on, surnames became distant marks,
They began to scatter among the people, blending into ordinary streets and alleys,
Stretching out tentacles to deeper, farther, and more hidden corners,
On riverbanks, lake shores, embankments, and under eaves.

That sorrow from the marrow of the bones, in this world,
Cannot be raised up; one must lower the posture, lower it even further.
But they forgot— the true spirit of nobility
Cannot be concealed. When you open
The door to the white jade-like flesh, the kernel of life within.

December 18, 2020

三棱鏡

從一個側面望過去
每個人有無數個顯影
和三棱鏡相似
不同角度的光譜
還原成三顏色,才能還原
一個人在湖面上的影像
語言只是一個通道
湧入堅硬的潮水
在它們的另一個空間
肉體帶著自身的重量
從星空流螢一樣墜落
內心的原初,在鏡子的反面
它的光,被黑暗吞噬
那時,還沒有一雙慧眼出現

2021 年 1 日 25 日

Triangular Prism

Looking from one side,
Each person has countless reflections,
Similar to a triangular prism,
Spectrums of light from different angles
Must be restored into three colors to restore
One's image on the surface of a lake.
Language is just a passage,
Surging into the hard tides,
In their other space,
The body, bearing its own weight,
Falls like fireflies from the starry sky.
The primal core within, on the opposite side of the mirror,
Its light swallowed by darkness.
At that time, no discerning eyes had yet appeared.

    January 25, 2021

Hawking

坐標上，世界有兩個方向
肌體在逆行，宇宙在循環
物理學有兩個體系，物理系
霍金系。假如，假如是氣體
他就是氣體中最活躍的分子
世界恒量，宇宙變量
霍金才是變量中的變量

星雲無際，黑洞有界
在不可捉摸的地方打開深鎖的重門
那個預言人類黑匣子的人
沒想到，有人撬開了一道縫
而聯通了一條路。暗物質
黑暗星雲遙不可及。在地球
成為火星之前，時光彎曲
霍金，成為最後一顆發光的星球

2021年2月4日

Hawking

On the coordinates, the world has two directions,
The body moves in reverse, the universe cycles.
There are two systems in physics, the Physics system
and the Hawking system. If, if it were gas,
He would be the most active molecule in the gas.
World constants, cosmic variables,
Hawking is the variable among variables.

The nebula is boundless, the black hole has limits.
In the ungraspable, deep locks are opened,
That prophet of humanity's black box
Did not expect someone to pry open a crack,
Connecting a path. Dark matter,
The dark nebula, unreachable. On Earth,
Before it becomes Mars, time bends.
Hawking, the last glowing planet.

  February 4, 2021

內心的懸崖

從草屋出發,獵人的命運
就成為謎語,或者板上之釘
斧柯在你的手裡,蝕盡
從此獵人就活在各人的意念裡
大路朝天,不管你先邁左腳
還是右腳,無一例外
最終人們都會發現
你被困在自己或者別人的陷阱裡
一年復一年,一日復一日
你起早貪黑,給自己也給別人
設置各種懸崖,深入迷中
和我喜歡解數理,研究懸疑一樣
在一個又一個懸崖中
你把自己不斷推倒,或重構

  2021 年 3 月 30 日

Inner Cliff

Starting from the grass hut, the hunter's fate
becomes a riddle, or a nail on the board.
The axe handle in your hand, corroding,
From then on, the hunter lives in the minds of others.
The road leads to heaven, no matter whether
you step with the left foot or the right, no exception.
In the end, people will find
you trapped in your own or someone else's snare.
Year after year, day after day,
you rise early and toil late, setting cliffs for yourself and others,
delving into confusion.
Like my love for solving math and studying mysteries,
in one cliff after another,
you continually push yourself down, or reconstruct.

    March 30, 2021

過 虎 門

懾于它的威名
隔江，我就感受它
威逼的氣勢
一群捋虎鬚的人
打了個結，是為虎門大橋
車過橋心，咆哮的珠江
是一萬匹餓虎在嚎叫
江風獵獵，拂過橋索
如隱隱的群嘯之聲
你在一顆顆虎齒間數過
長安回望，深深地吸了口氣
在江流摧枯的門邊
你又一次，虎口餘生

2021 年 4 月 13 日

Crossing Humen

Trembling at its renowned might,
Across the river, I feel its
pressing force.
A group of men tugging at tiger whiskers
tied a knot, for the Humen Bridge.
As the car crosses the bridge's heart,
the roaring Pearl River,
a thousand hungry tigers howl.
The river wind sweeps past the bridge cables,
like the faint echo of a wild roar.
You've counted, between each tiger's fangs,
Long'an in your gaze, deeply inhaling.
By the river's edge, where the waters ravage,
once again, you survive the tiger's mouth.

    April 13, 2021

平 衡 術

我左眼的高處,常在雲端
自由往來。目之所見
無非邏輯,規律,公理
還有大勢和格局
和左邊不同
我的右眼高度近視
有時看見蚊子比磨盤大
有時一幢房子比針眼還小
左眼和右眼總是不服氣
所以,你看見我的時候
我不是閉著左眼
就是閉著右眼。總之
一定得閉上一隻眼

2021 年 5 月 26 日

The Art of Balance

My left eye often soars,
high above the clouds,
freely navigating. What I see
is nothing but logic, order, axioms,
the greater trend and pattern.
But unlike the left,
my right eye is nearsighted,
sometimes seeing mosquitoes bigger than millstones,
sometimes a house smaller than a needle's eye.
The left and right eyes can never agree.
So, when you look at me,
I'm either closing my left eye,
or closing my right eye.
In any case,
one eye must be closed.

    May 26, 2021

一枚蛋殼的安穩現世

我把它們，一片片
從蛋清的肉體上剝下來
一一擺放，像一個將軍
檢閱他疲憊的士兵
將軍不知道，每一個士兵的心裡
都有一道長長的裂縫

然後，我又將它們一一拼接
多麼完整的世界
就像當初天地未開的模樣
螞蟻，飛鷹，月亮和火星
定時從它的身邊起落
沒人知道，這個渾圓安穩的現世
是我用明膠粘起來的

  2021 年 6 月 8 日

The Stable World of an Eggshel

I peel them, piece by piece,
from the body of the egg white,
placing them one by one, as a general
inspects his weary soldiers.
The general doesn't know that in every soldier's heart
there lies a long, deep crack.

Then, I carefully piece them together,
such a complete world,
just like when heaven and earth were first formed.
Ants, eagles, the moon, and Mars
rise and fall in their regular rhythm.
No one knows that this round, stable world
was pieced together by me,
using nothing but gelatin.

    June 8, 2021

平行的世界

一位母親，在她折身的當兒
兩個人，最後
一個影子走出了地鐵口

天空裡飛行的不止是鳥
還有信
只是收信的人
在牆上，望著他笑了好多年

床病了，照顧它
這個老人，十年也未離開半步
愛情，有時候在肉體之外

白衣寺，鴿子叫了兩聲
城南，砌磚的工匠從牆頭落下
馬駒，從阿爾泰山站起來

2021 年 7 月 21 日

Parallel Worlds

A mother, at the moment of her turning,
two people, in the end,
one shadow walks out of the subway entrance.

In the sky, it's not only birds that fly,
but also messages.
Yet the one who receives them
has been smiling at the wall for many years.

The bed is ill, care for it.
This old man, has not moved a step in ten years.
Sometimes, love exists beyond the body.

At Baiyi Temple, a pigeon coos twice,
in the southern part of the city,
a bricklayer falls from the wall.
A horse, rises up from the Altai Mountains.

    July 21, 2021

大 鳥

它瘦得只剩一副爪子
和幾節骨架
每天夜裡它都要給自己
加兩節骨頭,以適應
樓群的高速生長
它在藍空裡,揮動著
它巨大的爪子
像一隻老鷹,築巢時
把周圍的樹木,雜草
泥巴,石塊,鋼條
和那些遊走的兩腳獸
都扒拉到自己窩裡
從我移居的火星角度看
大鳥棲息的球體
就是一個大蜂窩

2021 年 8 月 26 日

The Great Bird

It's so thin, only a pair of claws
and a few fragments of bones remain.
Every night, it adds two more bones to itself
to adapt to the rapid growth of the tower clusters.
In the blue sky, it waves
its massive claws,
like an eagle, when building its nest,
sweeping up surrounding trees, weeds,
mud, stones, steel bars,
and those two-legged beasts that wander about,
dragging them into its den.
From the perspective of Mars,
where I now reside,
the sphere where the great bird roosts
looks like a giant beehive.

    August 26, 2021

河流的一部分

他每天和太陽一樣準時
出現在河岸上
他種姜苗，種豆角，種花生
他也收割油菜，西紅柿和大白菜
日子是固定的，勞作是固定的
他的一生也固定在河岸
有時他是河的一部分
像河開出的一條支流
有時候，河也是他的一部分
是他的另一條胳膊另一個替身
河替他帶走了辛勞沉默和固執
也為他撫平內心的皺紋
他們彼此憐惜，疼痛和撫慰
他們時有分歧又時常交匯

2021 年 9 月 15 日

A Part of the River

He shows up every day, like the sun,
punctual on the riverbank.
He plants ginger shoots, beans, and peanuts,
and also harvests rapeseed, tomatoes, and cabbages.
His days are set, his work is set,
and his life is anchored on the riverbank.
Sometimes, he is a part of the river,
like a tributary that flows from it.
At other times, the river is a part of him,
his other arm, his alternate self.
The river carries away his labor, silence, and stubbornness,
and smooths the wrinkles of his soul.
They pity each other, in pain and comfort,
sometimes diverging, yet often converging.

    September 15, 2021

殘雪(1)的城堡

沒有門，你看見的門
是一幅抽象畫
隨著時間，溫度和季節
不斷變遷。也沒有路
你可以飛，可以拉著一個
影子和衣袖進入
當你放棄尋找，放棄希望的時候
腳下一滑，門開了
你看到一個不是城堡的城堡
不是自己的自己
望著自己，你就能看見
那是一頭熊，是一隻狼

當然，每一個人都是形狀不同的城堡
互不聯網。城堡的主題是戰爭與和平
孤獨的星辰沿著各自的路徑
擦肩而過，或稍許停留
互相深入，或矛刺相見
沒門的地方才是門
沒路的地方才是路
沒人的地方，人頭攢動

2021 年 10 月 7 日

註釋：(1)，殘雪，中國當代先鋒派文學代表作家，多次入圍國際布克獎。

The Castle of Can Xue

There is no door. What you see as a door
is an abstract painting,
changing with time, temperature, and seasons.
There is no path.
You can fly, you can take a shadow and a sleeve with you,
and enter.
When you stop searching, when you give up hope,
your foot slips, and the door opens.
You see a castle that is not a castle,
a self that is not your own. Looking at yourself, you see
it's a bear, it's a wolf.

Of course, everyone is a castle of different shapes,
interconnected, yet not. The theme of the castle is war and peace.
Lonely stars pass each other
along their own paths,
or pause for a moment.
They dive deep into each other, or their spears meet.
The place without a door is the door,
the place without a path is the path,
the place without people is crowded with heads.

    October 7, 2021

Note:
(1) *Can Xue* (残雪) is a Chinese contemporary avant-garde writer and one of the leading figures in Chinese literature. She has been nominated for the international Booker Prize multiple times.

小 廟

在半山，它那麼小
眾山明滅，燈火不彰
像個三尺高的袖珍模型
觀音佛只是個輪廓
渾圓如嬰孩
也許嬰孩才是佛的本體？
殘香幾枝，似是隨手所插
山深，水遠，廟小
遠山，近台，城廓
魂魄靈動
從那條小路曲折而來的我
千山萬水，也貢著一座小廟
我的肉身。一日三次的朝奉
歸了魚肉，納了山水
廟裡的真神，卻常常抽身

  2021 年 10 月 14 日

The Small Temple

On the half-mountain, it is so small.
The mountains flicker, the lights dim.
Like a miniature model, only three feet high,
the Buddha's figure is merely a silhouette,
round like a newborn child.
Perhaps the child is the true form of the Buddha?
A few branches of lingering incense, seemingly casually placed.
The mountain is deep, the water far, the temple small.
The distant mountains, the nearby platform, the city's corridors,
the soul stirs.
From that winding little path, I come,
through a thousand mountains and rivers, bearing a small temple,
my flesh and blood. Three times a day, I offer my devotion,
returning to fish and meat, accepting the mountains and waters.
Yet, the true god of the temple often withdraws.

    October 14, 2021

長日將盡

一條河寂寞地想著心事
我們也是
想著想著就擱淺了
岸上，魚群的骸骨
搭起層層樓閣
林蔭像描眉的女子
愈來愈潦草。她早已丟失了
那份堅持，草草收場
每一隻回到小巷的小獸
都是一個孤兒，從一個陷阱
跳進另一個陷阱
放火的人，搖動手裡的機關
穿著鋼鐵的外套
在火堆裡，放起了黑白片

2021 年 11 月 16 日

The Long Day Is Ending

A river silently ponders its thoughts,
and so do we.
As we think, we become stranded.
On the shore, the bones of fish
build layer upon layer of towers.
The tree shade, like a woman drawing her brows,
grows increasingly careless. She has long lost
her persistence, wrapping things up hastily.
Every little creature returning to the alley
is an orphan, leaping from one trap
into another.
The one who sets the fire shakes the mechanism in his hand,
wearing a steel coat,
and in the flames, plays a black-and-white film.

    November 16, 2021

在濕地公園

心若潮濕,就和植物們
扭纏不清。你無法清楚知道
每一棵水草的門楣
和它複雜的生世密碼
沒有一條水道有明確的指向
就像迷失在荷塘裡的我們
是並立的水蓮
還是倒伏在寒澤裡的燈芯草
在濕地,我們總是一次又一次
不斷追問和追認
每一個植物的身份與家譜
是來自海水還是陸地,或者
我們和兩棲的青蛙
是來自同一個家族。在濕地
唯一清楚的事實是
生與死,顯和隱,大象無形

2021 年 12 月 6 日

At the Wetland Park

When the heart is damp, it becomes entangled
with plants. You cannot clearly understand
the threshold of each water plant
and its complex life code.
No waterway leads anywhere with certainty,
just like us lost in the lotus pond—
Are we standing as water lilies,
or lying prostrate in the cold marsh, like bulrushes?
In the wetland, we keep asking and re-confirming
the identity and genealogy of every plant—
Is it from the sea or the land? Or
are we, along with the amphibious frogs,
from the same family? In the wetland,
the only clear fact is
life and death, appearance and concealment,
the elephant has no shape.

    December 6, 2021

摩崖石刻

人形還沒有出來
尚有一顆咆哮之心
每一個人都在獸和人
人和佛的巷子裡奔跑

一棵草一根樹杈一綹毛髮
漫不經心地搭著
隨意裡透著如此精心
它們的另一頭，開始凸現

每一個念頭都猶疑不定
同志們，鳴蟲，猛獸和飛禽們
從草屋出發吧
在文明的曙光升起之時，遠征

    2021 年 12 月 20 日

Inscribed on the Cliff

Before the human form emerges,
there is still a heart that roars.
Everyone runs in the alleyways of beast and human,
of human and Buddha.

A blade of grass, a branch, a strand of hair,
casually placed,
yet within the casual, there is meticulous intent.
On the other side of these, things begin to emerge.

Every thought is hesitant, uncertain.
Comrades, chirping insects, fierce beasts, and birds,
set forth from the grass hut.
At the moment when the dawn of civilization rises, embark on your expedition.

    December 20, 2021

卷六

落草記

石榴坑這麼深,不少人
生生世世也沒有爬出來過
在坑裡掙扎了半晌,扯著繩子
才攀上了六十度的坑緣
如果從大尖山的雲層裡
層層下落,北崖,馬蹄水
古香林,一直到賊老窩
你就從仙境,廟堂,江湖
成了一回草莽英雄
叢叢的竹林,透著重重山影
高岸的松陣,樹起森森刀劍
莢英,翠葉,落羽
山杜鵑,山茅草,千頭菊
共同圍成一個溫柔陷阱
一點一點地陷進去
在每一個岔路口,我總是努力
把自己,從懸崖邊撈起來

2022 年 1 月 10 日

Fall into the Grassland: A Record

The pomegranate pit is so deep, many people
have struggled all their lives and never climbed out.
After struggling for a long while in the pit, pulling on the rope,
I finally managed to climb the steep edge at a sixty-degree angle.
If you descend layer by layer from the clouds above Dajian Mountain,
past the North Cliff, Ma Ti Shui, and the ancient fragrance forest,
all the way to the bandits' den,
you would transform from a celestial realm, a temple, a world of rivers and lakes,
into a grassland hero.
The dense bamboo forests cast heavy shadows of the mountains,
the tall pine formations stand like an array of swords,
with pods, green leaves, falling feathers,
mountain rhododendrons, mountain grasses, and thousand-headed chrysanthemums
forming a gentle trap.
Bit by bit, I fall deeper and deeper into it.
At every fork in the road, I always try my best
to pull myself away from the edge of the cliff.

    January 10, 2022

春夜塤事

燈火晃了幾晃，熄了
說話的聲音漸漸弱下去
小下去。杯中酒，餘味
欲斷，還斷

雨水是一場暗戀
有些人，只能在黑夜裡掩面
春水，涮啊涮

春天把自己深埋下去
斑茅草冒出來
奶漿菜冒出來。比他更早的
黃醃菜，腰杆直了

隔著春簾，每喊一聲
綠帛上，我的影子就濃幾分

2022 年 2 月 16 日

Spring Night's Confessions

The lights flickered a few times, then went out.
The sound of conversation gradually weakened,
growing smaller. The wine in the cup, its aftertaste
wants to break off, but cannot quite break.

The rain is a secret love affair,
Some people can only cover their faces in the dark of night.
The spring water, washing and washing.

Spring buries itself deeply,
while the spotted grass sprouts,
and the milkweed comes up. Earlier than them,
the pickled mustard greens stand tall.

Behind the spring curtain, with every shout,
on the green silk, my shadow grows a little darker.

    February 16, 2022

人間薄事

橫樑山是一匹厚磚
上面爬滿了螞蟻的鄉親
麻雀和烏鴉各自安生
疼痛像刀片
遊走在生活之湖的水面
紅蜻蜓棲在艾葉上
黃色的風攪動著浩蕩的麥芒
牛犢像個孤雛
在刺笆叢裡伸出小黑頭
裹著頭巾的人
從白天走到黑夜,僅僅是
從紙的正面走到背面

2022 年 3 月 2 日

Trivial Matters of the World

Mount Hengliang is a thick brick,
covered with the ants of the village.
Sparrows and crows live in peace.
Pain moves like a blade,
wandering on the surface of life's lake.
Red dragonflies rest on mugwort leaves,
and the yellow wind stirs the vast wheat awns.
The calf, like a lone chick,
pokes its little black head out from the thorny bushes.
People with headscarves
walk from day to night,
simply moving from the front of the paper to the back.

March 2, 2022

風語者

一場大雨之後,小巷,碼頭,桅檣,寺廟
迎來了一場異型木棉的白色飛絮
它們不斷地起落,飄浮,或者在發梢
掛著。在飛鳥的翅膀小牯牛的角尖晃動
人間,是一場生命與生命的不斷接力
也是一片互相阻斷,各自為王的競技場
古老的藤蔓族們,緊緊地抱著松樹的軀幹
它亙古不變的愛,深深地勒進烏桕馬尾松
和木荷的肢體。那些互為世仇者
卻拓寬了森林家族最深的依存與榮辱之路
穿過風雨的人,必將付之於風雨
所有的秘密都在光天化日之下,每一次沖洗
都會將一些事物昭於天下,又將另一些用心
悄悄植入。那些被喚醒的事物終將
被自己埋葬,又會被繼任者再來一次證明

  2022 年 5 月 31 日

Wind Speaker

After a heavy rain, the alleyways, docks, masts, and temples
are greeted by the white fluff of the strange kapok trees.
They rise and fall continuously, floating, or hanging
on the tips of branches.
The wings of flying birds and the sharp horns of young calves sway.
Human life is an ongoing relay of lives,
and also a competitive arena, each struggling to dominate,
a field of mutual isolation.
Ancient vines tightly clasp the trunks of pine trees,
their eternal love deeply entwined with the branches of the Camphor pine
and the Molucca wood. These enemies,
have widened the path of the forest family's deepest bonds and honor.
Those who pass through wind and rain
will pay their price in wind and rain.
All secrets are revealed in the full light of day; each time they are washed,
some things will be exposed to the world, while others are quietly planted
with intent. The things awakened will ultimately
be buried by themselves, only to be proven again
by their successors.

May 31, 2022

群山之上

一步步從樹根,沙礫和鋸齒般的石縫裡
把自己挪上去。和那些茅草,野棘
木荷,假苹婆,陰香,稱星樹和鵝掌柴們
稱兄道弟。在山野,沒人認識你
顯赫的家世與名門。甚至你也是無名的
你的行走,並不能證明你的智慧
比一隻麻雀,山雞,或者石縫裡的一隻螃蟹

更多,更聰明。甚至,連一隻沒有出窩的雛鳥
也能對你嘶叫,示威。拆了利爪的人
再怎麼張牙舞爪,攻於心機,都是枉然
深入,就是從一個坑邁向更深的坑
就是一個人向一棵植物慢慢轉化
山峰邁向山峰,一點一點地交出翅膀
群山之上,只宜赤誠相見
群山的寬衣袖袍和皺褶紋理
甚至那些玄武紀的岩石,光滑的胸肌
像一個人,為你除下了它所有的裝飾物
群山之上,最合適的慷慨
是把自己,交給一隻凌空而過的鷂鷹

2022 年 6 月 20 日

Above the Mountains

Step by step, from tree roots, gravel, and jagged rock crevices,
I move myself upward. Alongside the reed grass, wild thorns,
camphor trees, false water plantains, shadow flowers, star trees,
and goosefoot shrubs,
we become sworn brothers. In the wilderness, no one knows you,
your distinguished ancestry or your noble lineage.
Even you are nameless.
Your journey does not prove that your wisdom
is greater than a sparrow, a pheasant, or a crab in the rock crevices.

More, more clever? Not even a chick that hasn't left the nest
can't hiss at you in defiance.
Those who have had their claws removed,
no matter how they try to claw, scheme, or attack, it's all in vain.
To go deeper is to move from one pit to an even deeper pit,
to transform from a person into a plant.
Mountains rise towards mountains, piece by piece they surrender their wings.
Above the mountains, sincerity is the only way to meet.
The wide sleeves and folds of the mountain's robe,
even the ancient rocks of the Pre-Cambrian period, the smooth chest muscles,
are like a person who removes all their adornments for you.
Above the mountains, the most fitting generosity
is to give yourself to a kestrel soaring through the air.

    June 20, 2022

紙上河流

說到河流，波浪就湧上來
月光濺在紙上，濡濕了整個唐朝

流逝的影子，疊起來
是一座從山海關延綿到天山的長青林

故人何處，一塊麻石
只能在河流的最深處，安身

翻過這一頁，整個南嶺壓至城樓
螻蟻們，密密麻麻地立在珠江

此去，長路有多少曲折
我，就有多少悲傷，瀝過紙背

2022 年 7 月 8 日

Paper Rivers

Speaking of rivers, waves surge forth.
Moonlight splashes onto the paper, soaking the entire Tang Dynasty.

The shadows of time, stacked upon each other,
form a lush forest stretching from the Shanhaiguan Pass to the Tianshan Mountains.

Where is the old friend? A piece of rough stone
can only take refuge in the deepest part of the river.

Turning this page, the entire Nanling Range presses down upon the city walls.
Ants, thick and dense, stand on the Zhujiang River.

From here onward, how many twists and turns the road holds,
there will be as much sadness as I leave behind, seeping through the back of the paper.

    July 8, 2022

雨夜寫給卡夫卡

路上很擠，落葉，鐵銹
語言的碎片，殘肢的人偶
用力要喊出疼痛的石頭雕像
殘山剩水，沒有同行者
在前來的路上
那些凝固的胃攪動著大地的神經
卡夫卡，穿過這雨幕
我要為面具找到臉龐
為思想找到頭顱
為木頭找到愛情
為雨水找到歸處
然後，我再從雨水中活過來

  2022 年 8 月 4 日

A Rainy Night Letter to Kafka

The road is crowded, with fallen leaves, rust,
fragments of language, and the dismembered limbs of
mannequins.
The effort to scream through the pain, a stone sculpture.
Ruined mountains and remaining waters, with no companions.
On the way ahead,
the stomachs frozen in place stir the nerves of the earth.
Kafka, through this rain curtain,
I must find a face for the mask,
a skull for the thought,
love for the wood,
a home for the rain.
Then, I will emerge alive again from the rain.

    August 4, 2022

暮色裡的白鶴是一種隱喻

黃昏像一副翅膀落下
一群樹上的白鶴
在河岸上入定。似乎
要沉入暮色的深處
最後一抹夕陽的餘光
探照燈似的打在樹上
白鶴的羽毛
像灰屏上的亮色點陣
像素般拼成了一幅深景圖
所有的事物都被虛置
只有這些漂白之色
浮雕一樣，從暮色裡凸出來
而我，愈陷愈深

2022 年 10 月 14 日

The White Cranes in the Twilight are a Metaphor

The dusk falls like a pair of wings,
A group of white cranes on the trees
Enter stillness by the riverbank. It seems
They are about to sink into the depths of the twilight.
The last faint glow of the setting sun
Shines on the trees like a spotlight.
The feathers of the white cranes
Are like bright pixels on a gray screen,
A deep landscape image pieced together in pixels.
All things are rendered virtual,
Only these bleached colors,
Like a bas-relief, emerge from the twilight.
And I, sinking deeper and deeper.

    October 14, 2022

落在舊巢裡的雨水

城市掛滿了鳥巢
長脖子短脖子的鳥兒們
伸出頭,等著
太陽出來打開天空之鎖

雨水彙集,成為了群體事件
一段危險的旅行
在於歸來的途中
與雲霧,有多次的時空密接

大風們,一向居心叵測
煽動草木的不臣之心
落在舊巢的雨水們,窮盡一生
也無以自證,清白之身

    2022 年 11 月 8 日

Rainwater Falling in the Old Nest

The city is filled with bird nests,
Birds with long necks and short necks,
Stretching out their heads, waiting
For the sun to rise and unlock the sky.

Rainwater gathers, becoming a collective event,
A dangerous journey
That lies in the return trip,
With multiple instances of temporal and spatial proximity to clouds and mist.

The strong winds, always harboring ulterior motives,
Stir the rebellious hearts of grass and trees.
The rainwater falling in the old nests, after a lifetime,
Cannot prove its innocence,
Nor cleanse itself.

    November 8, 2022

誰 是 誰

我是機器是沙子是泡沫的部分
是石頭是城牆的神廟的部分
是物質的一部分也是反物質的部分
是黑洞是黑箱，也是反黑洞反黑箱
我是樹是鐵是流沙是旋渦是風暴
是看不見的也是看得見的
我是你丟失的那部分，也是
一個瓷瓶破碎，是眾神
拋棄和竭力尋找的那部分
在時間之外時間之內又是被時間
任意曲解，隨意塗抹的那部分
我是一棵香樟，一隻飛鷹
一個人內心的閃電，一場大雨
漏夜的奔赴。一場即將到來
卻永遠也不會到來的風暴前奏
我是囚徒也是囚籠
是一棵樹的因也是一棵樹最後的果

2022 年 12 月 12 日

Who Is Who

I am the machine, the sand, the part of the foam,
I am the stone, the temple of city walls, a fragment of home.
I am part of matter, part of anti-matter too,
I am the black hole, the black box, and the anti-black, the undo.
I am the tree, the iron, the drifting sand, the whirl, the storm,
I am the unseen, yet seen in every form.
I am the piece of you that was lost,
A shattered porcelain jar—the gods' own cost:
The part they abandon, yet strive to find,
Outside of time, within it, twisted and maligned.
I am a camphor tree, a soaring hawk,
A lightning strike within a human heart,
A midnight downpour, racing through the dark,
The prelude to a storm forever approaching,
Yet never arriving, endlessly encroaching.
I am the prisoner and the cage,
The cause of a tree, and its final fruitage.

December 12, 2022

藍色妖姬

煤氣嘶嘶地在暗中嘶鳴
天空濡濕的翅膀一樣
慢慢下垂
走過的腳步，像蒙著布的木棍
敲打著實心的地面
江面暗啞，曠野屏住呼吸
咖啡的氣味從玻璃牆中透出來
河岸，小亭，白皮屋
皮椅上
她把裙裾攤開，陷進去
灰白的霧氣裡
像一朵剛剛打開的藍色妖姬
仿佛一招手
她就能從浮雕中走出來

  2022 年 12 月 14 日

Blue Enchantress

The gas hisses in the dark,
like wings of the wet sky
slowly folding down.
Footsteps pass, like cloth-wrapped sticks
beating on solid ground.
The river lies muted, the wilderness holds its breath.
The smell of coffee seeps through the glass walls.
By the riverbank, a small pavilion, a white-washed house—
on the leather chair,
she spreads her skirt, sinks into it.
In the gray-white mist,
like a newly bloomed blue enchantress,
as if with a single wave of her hand
she could step right out of the relief.

  December 14, 2022

尋找博爾赫斯
（組詩）

"就像水消失在水中"[1]
　　　　　——題記

螺旋型圖書館（一）

空間是立體的，在運動中
沙子，礫石，鐵礦，草木，河山
毛髮和骨頭，霧氣與靈魂
以彼此的面目顯現
色彩因人而異，幻化無恒
每一本書都是一個無序的世界
自由生長或死亡
或遮蔽。靈魂像文字一樣
呼吸與行走。統一與混亂
在森林裡，路徑就是牆垣
打開一本書，就打開了宇宙之門
進入與走出，都是反向的
像一面鏡裡的層層疊影

Searching for Borges
(A Sequence)

"Like water disappearing in water"
—*Epigraph*

Spiral Library (I)

Space is three-dimensional, in motion—
sand, gravel, iron ore, plants, rivers, mountains,
hair and bone, mist and soul,
revealing themselves in one another's guise.
Colors vary by the observer, shifting, unsteady.
Each book is a chaotic world,
growing freely or dying,
or concealing itself. Souls, like words,
breathe and walk. Unity and disorder
in the forest, where paths are walls.
Open a book, and you open the door to the universe.
To enter is to exit; to exit is to enter—
like layers upon layers reflected in a mirror.

鏡 子（二）

昨天是亞歷山大
今天從藤床上翻過身子
又叫孔丘，走出了齊國大都
山河隆起，大地塌陷
昨天是鏡子的正面，今天是鏡子的背面
未來正從鏡子裡走出來
滿身毛髮的靈長動物
還是處子之身
把自己懸空，和世界一樣
倒著看，能看見靈魂如何飄移
如何從骨頭裡一點點流逝
像生活，如何吹幹一棵草芥的骨血

Mirror (II)

Yesterday was Alexander;
today, turning on the vine bed,
he is Confucius, stepping out of the capital of Qi.
Mountains rise, the earth collapses.
Yesterday was the mirror's front; today, its back.
The future walks out of the mirror,
a hairy primate,
yet still a virgin.
Suspended like the world itself,
seen upside down, one can watch the soul drift,
seeping from bone, bit by bit,
like life, drying out the marrow of a humble blade of grass.

結滿果子的樹（三）

我是那棵樹，是樹的影子與替身
也是一個皇權時代的代言
是森林和整個星系
所有的星星掛在夜晚的樹枝上
一顆星就是一個行走的亡魂
一棵樹也是一口棺材
裝滿了人類的泥胎
樹替人活著，人替樹死去
它們互為彼此，像一個星系的自洽
就像世界藏身於果實
就像我，隱身於一棵樹中
對了，我叫博爾赫斯
他從未見面的雙胞胎兄弟
是他的年青和老年

  2023 年 1 月 16 日

[1]. 引自博爾赫斯《另一次死亡》

Tree Laden with Fruit   (III)

I am that tree—its shadow, its surrogate.
I am also a voice of an age of empires.
I am the forest and the entire galaxy.
All stars hang on the branches of night;
each star, a wandering ghost.
A tree is also a coffin,
filled with the clay bodies of humankind.
The tree lives for man, man dies for the tree.
They are each other, a self-consistent galaxy,
as the world hides inside its fruit,
as I hide inside a tree.
Yes, my name is Borges—
his twin brother, never met,
his youth and his age.

  January 16, 2023

---

¹ *From Jorge Luis Borges, Another Death*

空 廟

石廟山,和
它的存在像它的歷史一樣可疑

廟在哪兒
一夥上山的人問我

轉過那個草坡
巨石前面就是了

下午
又在湖邊遇上同一夥人

那裡根本就沒有廟
他們遠遠地就朝我喊

你沒看見坐在石墩裡的佛嗎
我也大聲地問他們

2023 年 2 月 13 日

Empty Temple

Stone Temple Mountain, and
its existence as doubtful as its history.

"Where is the temple?"
a group climbing the mountain asked me.

Over that grassy slope,
in front of the giant stone, there it is.

In the afternoon,
I met the same group again by the lake.

"There's no temple there at all,"
they shouted from afar.

"Didn't you see the Buddha sitting on the stone block?"
I shouted back at them.

    February 13, 2023

困 境

轟鳴衝擊、包圍
壓迫著身體周圍的空氣
一隻鳥在金屬罩裡
用它寬闊而巨大的翅膀
振動。持續地穿透一切障礙物
共同構成諧振的屏障
碾壓，擠兌
喉嚨越勒越緊，你喊不出聲
繩子慢慢拉長
骨頭咔咔作響
靈魂像一道煙
瞬間，就要破壁而出
氣泡
一直卡在沸騰前的臨界點上

2023 年 3 月 10 日

Predicament

Roaring impacts, encirclement,
pressing on the air around the body.
A bird, trapped inside a metal dome,
beats its broad, enormous wings,
vibrating. Continuously piercing all barriers,
forming a resonant blockade.
Crushing, crowding,
the throat tightens, no cry escapes.
The rope slowly stretches,
bones creak and groan.
The soul, like a wisp of smoke,
for a fleeting moment,
is about to break through the wall.
Bubbles—
stuck, forever at the critical point
just before boiling.

    March 10, 2023

打開天窗說亮話

把飄窗推開，把門推開
把一切能推和不能推的門戶
都打開
從大漠跑過來的沙塵
撲向我們的懷抱
好像我們
是它前世的親人
卡爾維諾望著遠方，如有所思
博爾赫斯從開叉的小徑上
匆匆走來
馬爾克斯像一個回教徒
在掌上研究他的心靈地圖
他們都是敞亮的人
打開了很多的窗子和門洞
只是我們都在黑暗裡
用一些華麗的詞藻
壓住聚光燈下遊移的陰影

2023 年 4 月 13 日

Opening the Skylight and Speaking Clearly

Push open the bay window, push open the door,
open every portal,
whether it can be pushed or not.
The dust from the desert
rushes into our embrace,
as if we
were kin from its previous life.
Calvino gazes into the distance, deep in thought;
Borges hurries along a forked path;
Marquez, like a devout Muslim,
studies the map of his soul in his palm.
They are all people of light,
opening countless windows and doors.
Yet we remain in darkness,
pressing down the drifting shadows
under the spotlight
with ornate words.

    April 13, 2023

歷史事件

風扯得很緊,雪花們在天上開會
到底
要不要落下來,什麼時候落下來

樹捂著眼睛,貓捂住眼睛,天
也捂住眼睛
刀陣停止滾動,氣氛凝固

畫圖的人,依然專注於圖上
勞駕,挪挪你的劍,擋了我的光
他說

收筆
寒光閃動。畫面又翻了一頁

2023 年 4 月 26 日

Historical Event

The wind tugs tightly; snowflakes hold a meeting in the sky—
whether, after all,
to fall, and when.

Trees cover their eyes, cats cover their eyes, the sky
covers its eyes too.
The blade formations stop rolling; the atmosphere solidifies.

The artist, still focused on the drawing,
"Excuse me, move your sword—it blocks my light," he says.

Lower the brush.
Cold glints flash. The page turns once again.

    April 26, 2023

南方雨季

你的世界只有巴掌大
一頭縶進霧水裡
你就是游在森林裡的魚
冷不丁
就從霧水裡冒出一些怪鏡頭
一輛跌跌撞撞的電車
一棵影影綽綽的街樹
一堵黑森森的牆壁
一顆濕淋淋的腦袋
無一例外，他們都從水裡瀝出來
濕漉漉的
這時候你又發現
你也成了一條濕毛巾
內心，流趟著一條憂傷的河

2023 年 5 月 9 日

Southern Rainy Season

Your world fits in the palm of a hand.
Diving headfirst into the misty water,
you are a fish swimming through the forest.
Suddenly,
strange glimpses rise from the fog:
a jolting tram,
a street tree shrouded in shadow,
a dark, looming wall,
a dripping wet head—
without exception, they all seep out of the water,
soaked through.
At this moment, you realize
you have become a wet towel too,
and inside, a river of sorrow flows.

    May 9, 2023

神隱少女

我將在你們出生之前
提前出生。我也將在你們
歸去之後最後歸去

你看不見我
誠如你們看不見神
看不見心的居所，雨的靈魂
一個身體裡的異質者

你不知道我有多少對翅膀
就像我不知道
你昨天是一隻老虎還是一隻病貓
在風中的掙扎與撕裂

你讀出的每一種植物
都曾經是我身體的一部分
就像你看見的每一個我，都不是我
換一個身份，我將長生或者速朽

    2023 年 5 月 29 日

The Hidden One

I will be born
before you are born. I will also be
the last to depart, after you are gone.

You cannot see me,
just as you cannot see god,
cannot see the dwelling of the heart, the soul of rain,
the stranger housed within a body.

You do not know how many pairs of wings I have,
just as I do not know
whether yesterday you were a tiger or a sick cat,
struggling and tearing in the wind.

Every plant you are able to name
was once a part of my body.
Just as every version of me you see is not me.
Change one identity, and I will live forever—
or perish at once.

    May 29, 2023

看不見的閃電

她躲在角落裡。這個孩子
是一個流落異鄉的孤雛
塵滿面，鬢如霜
零落的夥伴走失在紅山文化裡
流浪和遷徙
磕破的皮肉，嘴唇，深深的豁口
信仰一步步坍塌

清水緩慢注入
水罐開始回望，鼓蕩，蘇醒
有形的事物和無限對視
在局促的胸腔
微沫顫慄，像隱身的閃電
一個新人，打開肉身

2023 年 6 月 6 日

Invisible Lightning

She hides in the corner. This child
is a lost fledgling in a foreign land,
dust on her face, temples like frost.
Scattered companions vanish into the Red Mountain culture—
wandering and migration,
scraped flesh, lips, deep gashes,
faith collapsing step by step.

Clear water slowly pours in;
the water jar begins to look back, to stir, to awaken.
Tangible things and infinity gaze at each other
within the cramped chest.
Tiny bubbles quiver, like invisible lightning—
a new soul, opening its flesh.

    June 6, 2023

大雨，過白衣古寺
（組詩）

一

誰在用雷霆之怒
揮動萬縷銀絲的鞭子
抽打著這些大地上的子民
樹木，山石，湖泊
樓角和寺廟
老牆上的垛堞
像個失意的孤寡之人
在雨中嚎啕
露出那口參差不齊的豁牙
我在車窗裡
也能感覺到他的顫動
天空不空，大地逐步收縮

Heavy Rain, Passing the Ancient White-Robed Temple
(A Sequence)

I

Who wields the fury of thunder,
flinging a thousand silver-threaded whips
to lash the earth's children—
trees, rocks, lakes,
corners of buildings and temples?
The battlements on old walls
wail in the rain like a lonely, desolate soul,
revealing uneven, missing teeth.
I sit in the car,
feeling their tremor.
The sky is not empty;
the earth gradually shrinks.

二

風掃長街，被沖散的人
像受驚的螞蟻
從一個巢穴，撲向另一個巢穴
立在門框的女人
一串又一串的驚呼
砸在水泥地上
濺起落葉和紙屑
寺外，兩個緊緊貼著牆壁的漢子
仿佛是兩個泥塑羅漢
一場雨
淹滅了佛門真相

II

Wind sweeps down the long street;
scattered people, like startled ants,
rush from one nest to another.
A woman stands in the doorway,
shouts erupt one after another,
smashing against the concrete,
stirring fallen leaves and scraps of paper.
Outside the temple, two men cling to the wall,
like two clay Arhats.
A rainstorm
drowns the truth of the Buddha's gate.

三

禪門深閉，像鎖住的眉頭
形跡可疑的雨
製造懸念
密度不僅僅存于思想的叢林
在雨中觀寺
如觀眾生
簷角是至高無上的虛空
白衣不白
用一件雨衣灰袍
為古寺，披上一種錯覺
仿佛一個老僧
正冒雨誦經

2023 年 6 月 8 日

III

The Zen gate is tightly shut,
like furrowed brows locked in thought.
Suspicious rain
creates suspense.
Density exists not only in the jungle of the mind.
Watching the temple in the rain
is like watching all sentient beings.
Eaves are the supreme void.
White robes are not white—
a gray raincoat drapes the ancient temple,
casting an illusion,
as if an old monk chants sutras in the rain.

June 8, 2023

卷 七

VOLUME VII

刨

如果天空倒過來，我也要刨上一遍
像這樣，仔細些
一點一點，鋤頭下去的角度，力度，方向嚴格一致
像寫字一樣，一筆一畫，嚴謹，用心，心手合一
上一鋤的邊角和下一鋤邊角循序而進
和你編籬笆，畫向日葵的方式同出一轍
把黑夜刨過來，把白天翻過去
直到你的信心
身體裡的養分，耐心，期待，夢想都流回大地
你也可以東一榔頭，西一錘子
有一搭沒一搭。和一個不相干的人
說你年輕時的輕狂，疏放，和粗枝大葉一樣
在我的身後，石頭堆積如山，有些東西閃閃發光
山巒的起伏線，像河流一樣蜿蜒
又像我們經過的歲月，總是若有若無
夏天越來越短，野草越長越長
在我走後那個秋天
在我刨出大地骨頭的秋天，高粱湧浪，稻穀滔天

2023 年 7 月 27 日

Digging

If the sky turned upside down, I would dig it over too,
carefully, like this, bit by bit,
the angle, force, and direction of the hoe strictly consistent,
like writing—stroke by stroke, precise, mindful,
hand and heart as one.
The edge of one stroke flows into the next,
just like weaving a fence with you,
or painting sunflowers—the method the same.
I turn over the night, flip over the day,
until your confidence,
the nourishment, patience, expectation, and dreams in your body,
all flow back into the earth.
You can hammer here, hammer there,
sporadically, with someone unrelated,
telling of your youthful recklessness,
your freedom, as rough and unrefined as the branches.
Behind me, stones pile up like mountains, some things glimmer.
The undulating lines of the hills twist like rivers,
like the years we pass through—
always there, yet barely seen.
Summer grows shorter,
wild grass grows ever taller.
In the autumn after I leave,
in the autumn when I have dug out the bones of the earth,
sorghum surges, rice waves like a tide.

    July 27, 2023

困在語言的繭房

你搏擊，掙扎，一次次發起衝鋒
愚公移山一樣
一點點突破，移動，在語言的邊界裡
開疆辟土。奔跑，騎馬，禦風
你手中武器越來越多，越精良
你雄心萬丈，你意氣風發
破壁，突圍，在沙漠裡，在戈壁上
恣意縱橫，展開你強有力的翅膀
在語言的覆蓋之下
樹木活過來，群鹿在奔逐，牛羊繁衍
在這誕生的搖籃，搏殺的疆場
你因之而生，而苦，而累
也因之而榮，而樂，而憂
你就是你的上帝，語言的創造者，經緯編織人
你強大，成長和壯闊
語言也開始自我覺醒，壯大，生長，自我繁殖
你們同體共生，氣息相連
你餵養著它，它駕馭著你
你們互為良人，也是彼此的敵人
你是它的繩，也是它的筐
它是你最後的邊界，也是你最終的繭房

2023 年 8 月 29 日

Trapped in the Cocoon of Language

You strike, struggle, charge again and again,
like the Foolish Old Man moving mountains,
bit by bit breaking through, advancing,
opening new territories at the borders of language.
Running, riding, taming the wind,
your weapons grow in number and sophistication.
You are ambitious, full of vigor,
breaking walls, bursting through,
in deserts, on the gobi,
recklessly soaring, spreading your mighty wings.
Under the cover of language,
trees come alive, herds of deer run, cattle and sheep multiply.
In this cradle of birth, this battlefield of struggle,
you live, suffer, grow weary,
yet also gain honor, joy, and sorrow.
You are your own god,
the creator of language, the weaver of its warp and weft.
You are powerful, expanding, magnificent.
Language awakens, grows, reproduces,
breathing in tandem with you.
You feed it, it guides you.
You are each other's partner, and each other's enemy.
You are its rope, its basket;
it is your final boundary, and your ultimate cocoon.

August 29, 2023

自由的境界

小葉欖仁
豎起了一座綠色的金字塔
每到一定的高度
它就撐起密集的枝條
像撐開了一面圓傘
隔一定的高度，又長出一層
大傘，小傘，更小的傘
疊疊而上，每一部分
都是對自我的複製
枝條們，遵循著一種法則和韻律
平行，並列，整齊劃一
個性舒張，又群體協調
生命的最高自由
是對欲望和自我的控制
與約束

2023 年 9 月 11 日

The Realm of Freedom

The little-leaf elm
raises a green pyramid.
At a certain height,
it lifts dense branches,
like opening a round umbrella.
At another height, another layer grows—
large umbrellas, smaller umbrellas, even smaller ones,
stacked upward.
Each part is a copy of itself.
The branches follow a law and rhythm:
parallel, aligned, precise.
Individuality expands, yet the group coordinates.
The highest freedom of life
is the control and restraint
of desire and self.

    September 11, 2023

山陽道·魏風之阮籍

河山依舊。山陽道暴曬在烈焰中
叔夜,我用我頭換你琴吧
趕到東市的阮步兵,終究遲了一步
這是一場沒有送別的送別
求仁的人,都有一付好心腸
放開駑馬的韁繩
竹林蕭蕭,每一個山影
都是一個個死去又活過來的壯士
壯士不懼死,壯士們啊最怕的是生
生在這曲折破碎的末世
生在這亂石嶙峋,濁流河斷的蓬山
他要用血,一步步灑完這無盡的山道
他要用骨頭,一寸寸堆滿這月下的竹林
直到路盡,人窮,月隱,神退
阮步兵拋下車轅,曠山,荒野
還家。他閉柴扉,煮山茅,借一把月光
洗了又洗,這裡裡外外潰敗的傷口
"每一塊磚頭都沁滿了鮮血"
在月光下,星光替他打開了兄長的家書
阮步兵,用雙手從自己的身體裡
掏出一條條絲線,掏出
一節節鎖鏈,一節節碎片般的肋骨

2023 年 10 月 8 日

Shanyang Road • Ruan Ji of the Wei Style

The rivers and mountains remain. Shanyang Road bakes under blazing flames
Shuye, let me trade my head for your zither
Ruan the infantry officer rushing to the eastern market—in the end, he was one step too late
This is a farewell without a farewell
Those who seek benevolence all possess a kind heart
Releasing the reins of the weary horse
The bamboo grove whispers and sways, each shadow of the mountain Is a warrior who died and lived again
Warriors do not fear death—ah, warriors fear most to live
To live in this twisted, broken end of an era
To live in these rugged, barren Peng Mountains, where muddy streams run dry
He will use his blood, step by step, to stain this endless mountain road
He will use his bones, inch by inch, to pile up this moonlit bamboo grove, Until the road ends, the man is spent, the moon fades,
the spirit retreats Ruan the infantry officer casts aside the carriage shaft, the barren mountains, the wilds
And returns home. He closes the wooden gate, boils wild herbs, borrows a handful of moonlight
Washing and washing these festering wounds inside and out
"Every brick is steeped in blood."
Under the moonlight, starlight unfolds for him his elder brother's letter
Ruan the infantry officer, with both hands, draws from his own body
Strand by strand of thread, draws out
Link by link of chains, rib by splintered rib
    October 8, 2023

山陽道·魏風之王戎

每一粒米，都要用力滋長
時光苦短，時不我待
做一個鑿壁偷光的人
不浪費上天給予的每一分天賦
時光不曾負了卿卿
時光又曾誤了卿卿
是一份光，就要發十分熱
沒人懂你，癡狂的執念
和對自我的吝惜
人不惜命，天就不假年
對自己下手要狠
對別人，留一份最大的寬慰
你就是那一粒米
餵飽一個王朝的饑腸
長大了的人，才能與一個時代
同興衰，共短長

2023 年 10 月 12 日

Shanyang Road • Wang Rong of the Wei Style

Every grain of rice must grow with effort.
Time is bitterly short; it waits for no one.
Be one who chisels the wall, steals the light,
wasting none of the gifts heaven has granted.
Time has never failed you,
yet time has once misled you.
One ray of light must shine with tenfold heat.
No one understands you—your obsessive fervor,
your frugality toward yourself.
If man spares not his life, heaven grants no long years.
Be ruthless with yourself;
to others, leave the greatest mercy.
You are that single grain of rice,
feeding the hunger of a dynasty.
Only those who have grown fully
can rise and fall with an era,
sharing its brevity and its length.

    October 12, 2023

看不見的世界

村口，鳳凰樹葉子無來由地舞動
它和大平洋深處的某個風暴
彼此呼應。目光之外的存在之物
不是遠親就是近屬
它們沒有邊界，互相交纏
深入對方的腹部
你的門就是我的庭堂
我的腦袋也是你的手臂
黑烏鴉哼起山歌
兔子的身上殘留著虎豹的身影
野雉的羽毛有著太陽的光輝
水珠逸出大海
很多年以後，每一個思想的腦袋上
都有一棵，開花的樹

  2023 年 11 月 18 日

The Invisible World

At the village entrance,
the leaves of the phoenix tree dance for no reason.
They echo a storm deep in the Pacific.
Existences beyond sight
are either distant kin or close kindred.
They have no borders, intertwining,
penetrating into each other's depths.
Your gate is my courtyard;
my head is also your arm.
Black crows hum mountain songs.
On the rabbit linger traces of tiger and leopard.
The feathers of wild pheasants shine with sunlight.
Water droplets escape from the ocean.
Many years later, on every thoughtful mind,
there grows a flowering tree.

    November 18, 2023

時間的齒輪

——寫給 Lee Smolin

流雲，飛鳥，高山，石頭和大柏樹
村莊，牛羊，池塘，河中的流水
窗，窗外的楓葉，房間的灶台
坐在桌前的我，手中的鋼筆和書本
從松鼠眼裡透出的光，還有
在唐朝瓷碗裡延續，並且還在延續
永遠沒有盡頭的那根鏈條
像一張矢量圖，對，是全息圖
每一個事物都是星空裡的一個浮點
它們用圖景，流變的故事和時間的拓片
從各自的位置綻放矢量的煙花
一種形態是另一種形態的衍射，迭加
它們是你手中的沙，它們
是你對過去和十萬年後某一時刻的命名
它們是那批奧林匹斯山上的眾神
也是你我他和若干個世紀後
太陽下底下另一批不規則形態的製造者

2024 年 2 月 26 日

The Gears of Time
—*For Lee Smolin*

Flowing clouds, flying birds, high mountains, stones, and ancient cypresses.
Villages, cattle and sheep, ponds, the water in rivers.
Windows, maple leaves outside, the stove in the room.
I sit at the table, pen and book in hand.
Light glimpsed through a squirrel's eye, and
that endless chain
continuing in Tang dynasty porcelain bowls,
still continuing, never reaching an end.
Like a vector map—yes, a hologram.
Every thing is a floating point in the starry sky.
They bloom vector fireworks from their positions
through landscapes, evolving stories, and time's imprints.
One form diffracts another, superimposes.
They are the sand in your hand.
They are your naming of the past
and some moment a hundred thousand years hence.
They are the gods on Olympus,
and also you, me, and him,
and, centuries later under the sun,
another batch of irregular forms in creation.

February 26, 2024

涸 河

面對涸河,像一個人
面對自己的衰老
一天天看著手上的血管,癟下去
春天的茅草掩上來
想捂住昨晚的心悸與不可言說的
秘密。此時
紫荊花,黃花風鈴,三角梅
像大街上穿紅著綠的人
用誇張和鮮明的對比
捂住了枯河,欲睜還閉的眼睛
只有那些石頭
多像這春天遲到的人間
露出它溫情下的頭角

2024 年 3 月 20 日

The Dry River

Facing the dry river, like a person
facing their own aging,
watching the veins in their hands sink day by day.
Spring's wild grasses rise,
trying to cover last night's palpitations
and unspeakable secrets.
At this moment,
redbud, yellow bellflower, bougainvillea,
like people on the street wearing red and green,
use exaggeration and vivid contrast
to cover the dry river, eyes half-closed, half-open.
Only the stones
so much like those late arrivals of spring
reveal the subtleties beneath their warmth.

    March 20, 2024

十面埋伏

大地是一口鍋，天空罩著穹形的鍋蓋
群山升起，我在鍋底
在升騰的煙霧裡
乞行。群山們向我壓過來
不管我是樹還是草
它們都要榨盡，最後一滴汁液

河流，仿佛是盤踞在我身邊的一條蛇
它帶走昨天的冰凌
又將我置身一個不透風的蒸鍋裡
山外之人，將我和那頭黑牛
那群順風俯耳的綿羊們
餃子一樣，投入沸騰的鍋中

我的骸骨，是一柄五千年後的標槍
獨自兀立著

  2024年4月25日

Ambush from Ten Sides

The earth is a pot, the sky its domed lid.
Mountains rise; I am at the bottom of the pot,
begging my way through the ascending smoke.
The mountains press down on me—
whether tree or grass,
they will squeeze out the very last drop of juice.

The river coils like a serpent around me,
carrying away yesterday's ice,
and placing me in a windless steam pot.
Outsiders, beyond the mountains,
toss me and that black ox,
those sheep obedient to the wind,
like dumplings into the boiling pot.

My bones—
a javelin five thousand years hence,
standing alone.

    April 25, 2024

挖 藥

廣場上，只剩下他倆
此刻，好像互換了身份
石頭裡的李時珍還活著
他卻成了雕塑
他微仰，側著臉
望著李時珍的上半身
保持這個姿態，一動不動
外部世界一片茫然
遠處，住院部的大樓隱入煙雨中
看那情形
他在固執地找著自己的答案
他要從李時珍的身上
挖出一味，救兒子的藥來

2024 年 5 月 30 日

Digging for Medicine

In the square, only the two of them remain.
At this moment, it's as if they have swapped roles:
Li Shizhen in the stone still lives,
while he has become the sculpture.
He tilts his head back,
turns his face sideways,
gazing at the upper body of Li Shizhen,
holding this posture, motionless.
The outside world is a blur.
In the distance, the hospital building
fades into mist and rain.
It seems he stubbornly seeks his own answer:
from Li Shizhen's body,
he must extract a remedy,
a medicine to save his son.

    May 30, 2024

挖 地 瓜

孩子們，是時候了
陽光將為你們揭開生活的全部真相
那些秘密通道即將關閉
你們得適應一個全新的世界
你們的一切，將成為另一些人的談資
底色，背景，或噪音
落葉是你們新生的禮花
死亡才是重生
洗盡泥沙少年的額頭
生活的坑，再一次填滿
你們留下的空，得很多年以後
才被人想起和銘記
我的宿命是
將你們挖出來，把自己埋進去

2024 年 6 月 12 日

Digging Sweet Potatoes

Children, the time has come.
Sunlight will reveal to you
the full truth of life.
Those secret passages are about to close.
You must adapt to a brand-new world.
All of you will become someone else's topic:
foreground, background, or mere noise.
Fallen leaves are your celebratory fireworks for rebirth.
Death alone is the true renewal.
Wash the mud from a boy's brow;
fill the pits of life once more.
The void you leave behind
will only be remembered and honored many years later.
My destiny is
to dig you out,
and bury myself within.

    June 12, 2024

落在寺頂上的雨

青雲寺端著身子
坐在雲堆裡
像一個坐懷不動的老先生

雨,變換著姿態和力度
用腳跟敲打腳跟的
節奏。在老先生的青皮上演奏

也有例外,在一條隊伍裡面
總有幾個激動分子
打錯節奏。成了寺裡的弦外之音

我更願意相信,雨
是一個掃地僧
讓我們的羞愧,一覽無遺

  2024 年 6 月 14 日

Rain on the Temple Roof

Qingyun Temple holds itself upright,
sitting amid the clouds,
like an old gentleman, unmoved in meditation.

Rain shifts its posture and strength,
tapping heel to heel,
performing on the old gentleman's green skin.

There are exceptions: in any procession,
a few excitable souls
strike the wrong rhythm,
becoming the temple's dissonant notes.

I prefer to believe the rain
is a sweeping monk,
laying bare our shame for all to see.

    June 14, 2024

秘密花園

鐮刀，一半隱於泥土
露在外面的那一半，開出一叢玫瑰

月光露出它的本相
口吃的人在花叢裡鼓動一陣陣蛙鳴

隱士們在花徑裡趕路
被蝴蝶追逐，我們舉缽齊眉，互為山水

據說，每一棵植物都是一個套娃
每打開一層，都會深入一步，如尋蓮蓬

歷史的秘密就如花瓣，每一層都是環扣
揭開蓋子的人，正捂住那只蓋子

2024 年 7 月 12 日

Secret Garden

The sickle, half buried in the soil,
the exposed half blooms into a cluster of roses.

Moonlight reveals its true form.
A stammering voice stirs
waves of frog calls among the flowers.

Hermits hurry along the flower path,
chased by butterflies;
we raise our bowls in unison,
becoming each other's mountains and rivers.

It is said every plant is a nested doll,
each layer opened takes you deeper,
like searching for a lotus seed pod.

History's secrets are like petals,
each layer interlocking;
the one who lifts the lid
is also covering it.

    July 12, 2024

秋聲唉鳴

千秋嶺是一個壯漢,氣力漸盡
露出它翠色下的杏黃旗
正如一個發跡之人
布袍之下,不時隱現錦衣一角
雄兵十萬,在嶺外整裝
西風在自己的營帳裡,厲兵秣馬
它的前鋒,已劍指關外

深山的鷓鴣長一聲短一聲
多像一個唱後庭花的人
秋蟬們是些走不出自我的搖滾歌手
熱辣辣的歌詞卻只有蒼涼
村莊裡進出的人們
一聲不吭,瘦硬的臉上皆是草木
樺樹上的烏鴉
為它的流亡,準備了最後的悼詞

2024 年 8 月 22 日

Autumn Cry

Qianqiu Ridge is a strongman,
his strength gradually fading,
revealing an apricot-yellow banner beneath the green—
like a man on the rise,
whose silk robe peeks from under coarse cloth.
A hundred thousand soldiers stand ready beyond the ridge.
The west wind, in its own camp, sharpens weapons and feeds the horses;
its vanguard already points the sword beyond the pass.

In the deep mountains, the partridge calls,
long then short,
like someone singing Houting Hua.
Autumn cicadas are rock singers
unable to escape themselves,
their fiery lyrics sounding only desolate.
Villagers come and go silently,
their thin, hardened faces overgrown with foliage.
Crows on birch trees
prepare their final lament for exile.

    August 22, 2024

瘦 金 體

你真是瘦呀
我擔心你咳一聲
會咯出一口北宋的血來
因為瘦
才有自己的硬度
從你的身上
我看到文天祥
和袁崇煥骨頭裡合金的份量
瘦，不是家國病
是一種壓縮
是把胸中的萬里河山，壓縮成
一根竹竿的銀鉤鐵劃

  2024 年 9 月 11 日

Slender Gold Script

You are truly slender.
I fear that if you cough,
you might spit out a mouthful of Northern Song blood.
It is because of your thinness
that you possess your own hardness.
From your body,
I see Wen Tianxiang,
and the alloyed strength in Yuan Chonghuan's bones.
Thinness is not a malady of nation or home;
it is compression,
pressing the vast rivers and mountains of your chest
into the silver hook and iron stroke of a single bamboo rod.

    September 11, 2024

坐在深秋的槐蔭裡

秋天是個很直接的人
熱情或者冷峻,都開門見山
坐在深秋的槐蔭裡
秋風還小心翼翼
生怕力度過猛,驚嚇了遠山近水
無聲之中,它將天空
越推越遠。像一個人的青春
遙不可及
坐在輪椅上的老嫗
一臉秋空般的平靜,悲喜無痕
身後的推車人
一隻病腿,踱一步,顛一下
黃昏越來越近
一高一低的影子,越來越淡

  2024 年 10 月 14 日

Sitting in the Shade of Locust Trees in Late Autumn

Autumn is a direct soul,
its warmth or chill laid bare at the gate.
Sitting in the shade of locust trees in late autumn,
the autumn wind moves cautiously,
afraid its force might startle
the distant mountains and nearby waters.
Silently, it pushes the sky ever farther—
like a youth
beyond reach.
An old woman in a wheelchair
wears the calm of autumn skies,
her joy and sorrow leaving no trace.
Behind her, the one who pushes the chair,
a sick leg steps, teeters.
Dusk draws nearer,
high and low shadows
fading more and more.

October 14, 2024

線 頭

睜大眼睛，用盡力氣
也找不到那根
自己埋進去，混進棘叢的線頭
而它並非有意將自己混跡於
人堆，或斑駁的舊時光
一個不願認輸的人
與線頭扭纏，鬥智又鬥勇
但我堅信，它走神的時候
經歷了眾多的失敗
你才有機會將它從紛亂的塵世裡
撈出來。就像你
於醉夢之中，從嘉陵江的涼水裡
撈出一輪明月

2024 年 10 月 21 日

Thread End

Eyes wide open, straining,
you still cannot find
the thread end
you buried yourself,
woven into the thorns.
Yet it did not intend
to hide among the crowd
or in the mottled past.
A person who refuses to yield
wrests with the thread end,
mind and courage intertwined.
I firmly believe that,
in its moments of distraction,
after countless failures,
you have the chance
to pull it from the chaotic world—
just as you,
in drunken dreams,
draw a bright moon
from the cool waters of the Jialing River.

  October 21, 2024

暮靄的思緒

它是這樣的從容
像一種思想與另一種思想體系的
彌散。從任意的角度與方向
牆角,草叢,樹冠,河汊,淺澤
如果它有舵,那它
一定有一組無所不能的萬向輪
在你和我們沒有到達之前
在歷史的謎團還如堅冰之時,抵達

作為一個觀察家,在一座山的視覺中
時間是跳躍式的。這只兔子
它只會停在手執青草的牧人身邊
在個體思域裡的暮靄
出於疏忽或無視,顯然它對此熟視無睹
而作為一棵樹
從生態學的倫理中我熟悉它的邏輯
就像黃昏摸透了落日的路徑

  2025 年 11 月 18 日

Thoughts in the Evening Mist

It moves with such composure,
like one thought diffusing into another system of thought.
From any angle, any direction—
corners, grass, treetops, river branches, shallow pools—
if it had a rudder,
it would surely possess
a set of omnipotent omni-wheels,
arriving before you and us,
before history's enigmas, still hard as ice.

As an observer, in the vision of a mountain,
time leaps. This rabbit
pauses only by the shepherd holding grass.
In the twilight of individual thought domains,
through oversight or disregard,
it apparently takes no notice.
And as a tree,
from the ethics of ecology, I understand its logic,
just as dusk
traces the path of the setting sun.

    November 18, 2025

維多利亞灣上空的鷹

滑過的波音客機，低下了高昂的頭
一隻鷹的翅膀覆蓋了幾個王朝的背影
太平山上的宮殿和旗幟已經變換
唯有紫荊廣場正在怒放
這朵別在維多利亞灣胸襟上的花朵
被一艘艘遠洋貨輪的笛聲喚醒
它在中環廣場上繞了一周
畫著螺旋型的連線不斷地升上去，升上去
連國際金融大廈也小得像一根柴棍
它肯定看見那些從皇后碼頭離去的身影
那些從尖沙咀渡海而去的人
懷抱著一個時代的悲愴
擁抱著另一縷南來的風潮
從上午到黃昏，它在高高的空中盤旋
像掛在太平山頂的落日，不忍卒去

2024 年 11 月 23 日

Eagle Over Victoria Harbour

A Boeing glides by, bowing its proud head.
The wings of an eagle
cast shadows over several dynasties.
Palaces and flags on Victoria Peak have changed,
but only the Bauhinia Square blooms in rage.
This flower, pinned to Victoria Harbour's chest,
is awakened by the horns of distant cargo ships.
It circles the Central Plaza once,
drawing spiral connections, rising and rising—
even the International Finance Centre shrinks to a stick.
Surely it has seen the figures departing Queen's Pier,
those crossing from Tsim Sha Tsui,
carrying the sorrow of one era,
embracing a new southern wind.
From morning to dusk,
it soars high above,
like the sunset hung atop Victoria Peak,
reluctant to leave.

November 23, 2024

縱 虎 者

立石為山，縱水成河
這十萬畝綠林
總有一個規矩的開端
荒野的路徑自由地延伸，開叉
從螻蟻到山體
沿著各自歧路交錯
天是一頂穹蓋。盡一己之力
籠著十萬隻箭，又擎著十萬柄盾
於斯，生即是死，死才是生
天道是雨水，一邊澆一邊滅
放生，是道之始，也是終
山林嘯聚，高低起伏，彼消此長
縱，即是擒。擒，是為縱
誰的內心，沒有縱過十萬隻猛虎？

2024 年 12 月 9 日

Releasing the Tiger

Stones stand as mountains, waters run as rivers.
In these hundred thousand acres of green forest,
there is always a rule-bound beginning.
Paths in the wilderness extend freely, branching—
from ants to mountains,
intersecting along their separate forks.
The sky is a vaulted canopy.
With all its might, it cages a hundred thousand arrows,
and lifts a hundred thousand shields.
Here, life is death, and death is life.
The way of heaven is rain:
it pours and extinguishes at once.
Releasing life is the beginning of the Way,
and also its end.
The forest gathers with roaring winds,
rising and falling, one fading while another grows.
To release is to capture;
to capture is to release.
Whose heart has never released
a hundred thousand fierce tigers?

December 9, 2024

卷 八

VOLUM VIII

落在阿爾卑斯山的雪

——致阿方斯·瓦爾德

鷂鷹的背影投射在雲端
河流向上
母親的村莊隱入花蕊
衣飾的棱角為冰雪所鏤
靈魂之箭
在阿爾卑斯群山之上
最硬的是雪。這溫軟的刀
鏤刻出歐洲大陸的骨架
雪中的杉樹變換著站立的方向
面對阿爾卑斯山
落在畫布上的雪越來越厚
雪域鄉關
滑雪手杖卷起的颶風
拂過你高高隆起的顴骨
那只紅色羚羊
正從勃朗峰上一躍而過

2024 年 12 月 18 日

Snow Falling on the Alps

—To Alphonse Walde

A falcon's silhouette casts across the clouds,
Rivers rise,
The village of my mother fades into flower petals,
The edges of garments carved by the ice and snow.
An arrow of the soul,
Above the Alps,
Where the hardest is the snow. This soft, sharp knife,
Carves the very skeleton of the European land.
The fir trees in the snow shift their standing directions,
Facing the towering Alps,
And the snow on the canvas thickens with each fall.
In the land of snow,
The skiing poles stir a hurricane,
Brushing against your high, prominent cheekbones.
The red antelope
Leaps across Mont Blanc,
In one graceful bound.

December 18, 2024

鑲在藤蔓上的星星

石凳微涼，夜色似一杯奶液
冬蟲們已入酣夢
弦月和太白，正毗鄰而居
它們也撤去了自己栽下的籬笆
冬天的藤蔓只剩下枝杆
像水墨上的虯枝圖
乾淨，疏朗，精神矍鑠
仰望那些大大小小的星辰
像初春貼在枝條上密集的苞芽
它們，是相伴我們多年的故人
回到生活的枝條上
再一次，洗去人間煙火

    2025 年 1 月 8 日

Stars Embedded in the Vines

The stone bench feels cool, the night like a glass of milk,
Winter insects have already fallen into deep slumber.
The crescent moon and Venus,
Now dwell side by side,
Their fences pulled away,
The winter vines now only bare branches,
Like ink-wash sketches of winding twigs—
Clean, sparse, and full of vitality.
I look up at those stars, big and small,
Like the dense buds clinging to the branches in early spring,
They are old friends who have accompanied us for many years.
Returning to the limbs of life,
Once again, they wash away the smoke and fire of the world.

January 8, 2025

布 偶 人

他好像活了過來
在剛剛種下的玉米地邊
肥大的衣袖
在風中翻飛。腦袋
也在左右不停地搖晃
那些喜鵲,麻雀,烏鴉和斑鳩們
都是他潛在的敵人
——正蟄伏在荊棘叢中
大概他正在某一個舞蹈的情節中
還沒有回到現實中來
還沒有被房貸,工作和病痛所擊垮
更大的可能是
他用翩翩的衣袖
為那些失去的歲月
和那些活著的皮囊們,招魂

    2025 年 2 月 7 日

The Puppet Man

It seems he has come to life,
By the freshly planted cornfield,
His large sleeves
Flapping in the wind. His head
Keeps shaking left and right,
The magpies, sparrows, crows, and pigeons—
They are his hidden enemies,
Lurking in the thorny bushes.
Perhaps he is still caught in some dance,
Not yet returned to reality,
Not yet crushed by mortgage, work, and illness.
More likely,
He uses his fluttering sleeves
To call back the lost years,
And the souls of those living bodies.

    February 7, 2025

離鄉的麻袋

它累了,爬在地板上
經歷了兩千公里的風霜與勞累
生活中,哪一個遠行者不是如此呢
它的纖維條縷分明
縱橫線交織清晰而均勻
這樣的質樸、純真
與遙遠的愛爾蘭羊毛布
有著趨近的氣質
鄉土般的成色與底蘊
和那些在高粱,玉米和大豆間
隱現的面孔
都是這片土地上,牽扯的血親

  2025 年 2 月 18 日

The Sack from the Hometown

It is tired, lying on the floor,
After enduring two thousand kilometers of wind, frost, and toil.
In life, which traveler is not like this?
Its fibers are clearly defined,
The crisscrossing threads even and smooth.
Such simplicity, such innocence,
Is akin to the distant wool of Ireland,
With the rustic quality and depth of the land,
And the faces that flicker between the sorghum, corn, and soybeans—
They are all kin, tied to this land by blood.

    February 18, 2025

空中樓閣

我坐在 33 樓的客廳
像坐在一個略有涼意的鳥窩裡
這時的我和樓閣
像浮在大海裡的一枚繭殼
風湧過來
樓群彼此湧動如波浪
像是從地上開出來的水蓮花
我們這些農民的孩子
在夢中，努力地扯著自己的頭髮
將裹滿泥土的身子拔離地面
此刻，乾淨的世界
只有我和你
就像電影裡的一對假人
夜霧，悄悄抹去了腳下的根基

2025 年 3 月 14 日

The Castle in the Air

I sit in the living room on the 33rd floor,
Like sitting in a slightly chilly bird's nest.
At this moment, I and the tower
Are like a cocoon floating on the sea.
The wind rushes in,
The buildings move like waves,
Like water lilies blossoming from the earth.
We, the children of farmers,
In our dreams, pull at our own hair,
Trying to lift our bodies, covered in earth, from the ground.
In this moment, the world is clean,
Only you and I,
Like two mannequins in a movie.
The night mist quietly erases the roots beneath our feet.

    March 14, 2025

泥菩薩過河

好多人看笑話
紛紛表示，泥菩薩過不了河
有人飲酒，更有人猜拳
泥菩薩們，志得意滿
他們坐頭等艙
開私人飛機，過了河，過了江
又大搖大擺，過了太平洋
泥土表皮下皆為純正的金身
看笑話的人
成了那個，最大的笑話

2025 年 4 月 14 日

The Mud Buddha Crosses the River

So many people watch the spectacle,
And laugh, declaring the Mud Buddha cannot cross the river.
Some drink, others play rock-paper-scissors,
The Mud Buddhas, full of ambition,
Sit in first-class cabins,
Flying private planes, crossing rivers, crossing seas,
Swaggering across the Pacific.
Beneath the mud surface, they are pure golden forms,
And those who laughed,
Become the biggest joke of all.

    April 14, 2025

在黑夜裡相聚

有些是明亮的，有些是暗淡的
還有一些人不明不暗
從互相敵對的陣營走過來的人
彼此對峙，又互為知己
有人從看得見的地方來
有人從看不見的地方來
在黑暗裡相聚
不管你來自天堂還是地獄
我們都互不算計
在這樣的氛圍下，魔鬼和天使
都用同一種水杯喝茶
也都用同一種腔調說話

2025 年 4 月 25 日

Gathering in the Darkness

Some are bright, some are dim,
And some are neither clear nor dark.
Those who come from opposing camps,
Face each other, yet are mutual confidants.
Some come from places visible,
Others from places unseen.
We gather in the dark,
No matter if you come from heaven or hell,
We do not scheme against one another.
In this atmosphere, both devils and angels
Drink tea from the same cup,
And speak with the same tone.

    April 25, 2025

拙 夫

不同的時間，總有不同的蜜峰
在發財樹上飛旋
從樹幹到葉柄，從葉柄到葉尖
從葉面上嗅過來
又從葉背面嗅過去
我十分好奇
它幹什麼呢？光光的樹幹和樹葉
沒有花，更沒有蜜

它和我一樣嗎？明知道今年將會大旱
明知道風暴將會來臨
我依然一鋤一犁，種下大豆和高粱
明知道，寫下十萬首詩
也換不了一個饅頭和一枚雞蛋
更無法，讓某一個人回頭

2025 年 4 月 22 日

The Clumsy Husband

At different times, there are always different peaks of honey,
Spinning around on the money tree.
From the trunk to the petiole, from the petiole to the tip of the leaf,
It smells from the surface of the leaf,
Then smells from the underside of the leaf.
I am very curious—
What is it doing? The bare tree trunk and leaves,
No flowers, and no honey.

Is it like me? Knowing full well that there will be a drought this year,
Knowing the storm is coming,
I still plow and plant, sowing soybeans and sorghum.
Knowing that writing ten thousand poems
Will not get me a steamed bun or an egg,
Nor will it make anyone turn back.

    April 22, 2025

慌亂的風

是的，那時的它是慌亂的
曠野寧靜，湖水甘心情願地蜷在
一個叫白沙灣的懷裡
小溪，依舊在抒情
慵散的人失去了遠方的追問
細碎的花指示著小徑去向
那時的風，像一次突然爆發
一頭撞向那輛高速行進中的火車
拐過黃花梨的林梢
又從兩幢樓宇的空隙中，跌跌撞撞
將某種不明的東西，撲倒
一個遺留在殘山剩水裡的人
突然心悸，慌亂
在一面鏡子之前，手足無措

2025 年 5 月 5 日

The Frantic Wind

Yes, at that time, it was frantic.
The wilderness was quiet, the lake contentedly curled
In the embrace of a place called White Sand Bay.
The creek still sings its lyrical song,
The disoriented ones lost the questions of the faraway,
Tiny flowers pointing the way down the path.
At that time, the wind was like a sudden eruption,
Colliding head-on with a speeding train,
Turning around the crown of the yellow pear tree,
Then crashing through the gap between two buildings,
Knocking down something undefined.
A person left behind in the remnants of mountains and water,
Suddenly overwhelmed by palpitations, frantic,
Standing before a mirror, unsure of what to do.

    May 5, 2025

眞 相

我在地圖上一節一節地摸索著
嘉陵江像彈簧
一圈一圈地繞下去
我碰觸了它澎湃力量的源頭

月光是一所美學學院
給槍管和刺刀鍍上厚厚的白銀
只有歲月的砂子
才能磨平，一個男人的骨頭

2025 年 5 月 16 日

The Truth

I fumble, section by section, on the map,
The Jialing River like a spring,
Winding round and round.
I touch the source of its surging power.

Moonlight is an academy of aesthetics,
Coating gun barrels and bayonets with thick silver.
Only the sand of time
Can smooth a man's bones.

    May 16, 2025

被掩埋的巨人

我們住在時間的斗篷裡
在生活的井窖中
互相掩護,暗通曲款
和背離我們的靈魂相戀相纏相執
意念的蜂巢分割著王國的疆土
一簞食引發的戰爭
如海嘯不斷地洗刷我們的榮耀和恥辱
記憶是身體的紋路
我們都無法認領這個遠方的親人
沿著這條隧道
你會在另一頭,遇見
那個赤身裸體的自己,或祖先

  2025 年 6 月 3 日

The Buried Giant

We live beneath the cloak of time,
In the well of life,
Covering for each other, secretly exchanging favors,
Romancing, entwining, and clinging to the souls that turn away from us.
The hive of thoughts divides the kingdom's lands,
A mere bowl of food sparks wars,
Like tsunamis, continuously washing away our glory and shame.
Memory is the pattern of the body,
We can never claim this distant kin.
Along this tunnel,
At the other end, you'll meet
Yourself, bare and naked, or your ancestor.

June 3, 2025

飛 行 術

卡爾維諾練習飛行術
他常常抽離身體
在都靈,在威尼斯流連不歸
聖萊莫的那些熱帶植物
向他拋出密集的勾子
隱去了從泥地上崛起的秘密
卡斯提格連小鎮上生活過的祖先們
都有一副飛離地中海的翅膀
作為一個藝術營造師
卡爾維諾的彈跳,有著驚人的爆發
幾何結構是飛行的塔基
或是彈射,或是回旋,或是拋物
把自己裝進炮膛
他從過去,射向遙遠的未來

2025 年 6 月 18 日

The Art of Flight

Calvino practiced the art of flight.
He often detached from his body,
Lingering in Turin, in Venice, never to return.
The tropical plants of Saint-Remo
Tossed their dense hooks at him,
Hiding the secrets rising from the muddy earth.
The ancestors who lived in the small town of Castiglion
Had wings that flew away from the Mediterranean,
As an architect of art,
Calvino's leaps had a remarkable burst of power.
The geometric structure is the foundation of flight,
Whether it's a launch, a spin, or a parabola,
He packed himself into a cannon's chamber,
Shooting from the past into a distant future.

    June 18, 2025

夜雨打濕的人間

大地的傷口在彌補
縫合
這個漏斗
總有一些人被過濾
又有一些人被留守
芒果們
像一枚枚懸著的隱喻
又像是吊著的頭顱
如我們
挽著枯黃的肉身
六月的夜雨
替我們
撕開了掖著的紙封

2025 年 6 月 17 日

The World Wet with Night Rain

The earth's wounds are healing,
Stitching up,
This funnel,
Where some are filtered out,
And some are left behind.
The mangoes,
Like suspended metaphors,
Or like hanging heads,
Like us,
Clutching our withered, yellowed flesh.
The night rain of June
Tears open
The sealed paper we've kept hidden.

    June 17, 2025

黃昏裡的哈耶克

天空是大腦的突觸
流動的金箔在黃昏裡散開
不是風,只是那些狂奔的野馬
不可收拾
不是黑暗帶來了光
而是因為光才有了黑暗
那些逆光飛行的人
終將為光所傷
眾多的俠客們都在禦風而行
囚籠即是自由
終其一生
作為一枚黑色的箭頭
他準確地射中了太陽的靶心

2025 年 7 月 24 日

Hayek in the Dusk

The sky is the synapse of the brain,
Flowing gold leaf spreads in the dusk.
It's not the wind, but those wild horses galloping,
Unruly,
It's not darkness that brings light,
But light that gives rise to darkness.
Those who fly against the light
Will ultimately be hurt by it.
The many knights ride against the wind,
The cage is freedom,
And in their lifetime,
As a black arrow,
They accurately strike the bullseye of the sun.

July 24, 2025

別有深意

爬上了馬桑樹的菟絲子
掐掉自己腳下的根莖
生活中到處都有背水一戰的人
放眼所及，每一個領域的公民們
都保持著絕對的參差之態
彼處的圓弧，此處的尖削
深綠與淺黃，絳紫與大紅
每一顆向上的頭顱
針式，舌狀，刀片，星球，火焰狀
都來自每一個卓爾不群的心靈
和天賦的獨特稟性
他們的群像之上，星辰閃爍江漢奔湧
每一片樸素的伸展
每一次自由的綻放，都另有深意

    2025年8月7日

There's More to It

The bindweed climbs the pomelo tree,
Pinching off the roots beneath its feet.
Everywhere in life, there are those who fight with their backs to the wall.
Wherever you look, the citizens of every domain
Maintain an absolute state of divergence,
The arcs there, the sharp points here,
Deep green and pale yellow, crimson and bright red.
Every upward-facing head—
Needle-shaped, tongue-like, blade-like, spherical, fiery—
Comes from each unique soul,
And from their innate, exceptional traits.
Above their collective figures, stars shimmer and the Yangtze flows,
Each humble stretch,
Each free bloom, carries a deeper meaning.

    August 7, 2025

隱匿的星辰

每一隻蜜蜂都自帶光芒
這些錦上的織工
是一枚枚迅急的梭子
將花朵，山峰，溪流彙編於圖上
這繁複疊加，甬道悠長
層層暗河樹枝一樣
佈滿這個遙遠的星球內部
每一棵樹，每一個人
都在向虛空，伸長自己的頭顱
從一個枝椏伸向另一個枝椏
更多的人都是客串，都是群演
是些遺失了姓氏的工蜂

  2025 年 8 月 11 日

The Hidden Stars

Each bee carries its own light,
These weavers on the brocade,
Are swift shuttles,
Compiling flowers, mountains, and streams into a pattern.
This complex layering, the long, winding corridors,
Like dark rivers and branches,
Fill the interior of this distant planet.
Each tree, each person,
Reaches toward the void, stretching their head,
From one branch to another.
Most people are cameos, extras,
Lost worker bees with no surname.

  August 11, 2025

路過的雨如此隱忍

"世間最大的美德不是釋放,是自恰"
——題記

它仿佛,仿佛收起了心中萬千的風暴
把自己內心巨大的悲傷
壓下來。像壓進
一串串要湧出來的泉流
嬗化是一種緩慢的化學反應
只有修煉得足夠輕盈,足夠瑩潔
使它們,都具有飛翔的質地
才能從漫天的純度中,釋放下來
實體的雨,是一場自我救贖
六月的狂飆,七月的洶湧
只有八月的雨,能把堅硬的電子
把關不住的凌厲
揉進去,按下去。循環,揉捏,氣化
以絲,以霧,以霾,以霞之姿
漫天揮灑
為孤獨者,失意者和卑微者,壯行

2025 年 8 月 19 日

The Passing Rain Is So Patient

"The greatest virtue in the world is not release, but self-consistency."
—*Inscribed*

It seems, it seems to have tucked away the countless storms in its heart,
Suppressing its immense sorrow,
Like pressing down
A series of springs that want to gush out.
Metamorphosis is a slow chemical reaction,
Only when one is light enough, pure enough,
Can it give them the texture of flight,
And release them from the sky's purest depths.
The tangible rain is a form of self-redemption.
The wild storms of June, the surging tides of July,
Only the rain of August can press the hard hail,
The uncontainable sharpness,
Into itself, pressing it down. Circulate, knead, vaporize,
In threads, in mist, in sleet, in the radiance of dawn,
Scattering across the sky,
For the lonely, the disheartened, and the humble, to march on.

August 19, 2025

秋後算帳

白雲壓在前山的眉梢
像一位悵然若失的皓首之人
風，不肯退場
還在樓宇間撕扯
這一畝之地，它留下太多心血與遺憾
在人間
總有一些彎道你無法轉還
還有那麼多的石頭
從我們指縫的流水中溜走
歲月假裝慷慨
如我一般傳習大肚裡的道場
就像傳說中的風暴
萬眾翹首，它卻再一次爽約
正如一個人的淋漓症，絕口不提

2025 年 9 月 26 日

Settling the Account After Autumn

White clouds press on the brow of the front mountain,
Like an old man, lost in melancholy.
The wind refuses to leave,
Still tearing through the buildings.
On this patch of land, it has left too much blood and regret.
In life,
There are always curves you cannot turn back from,
And so many stones
Slip away through the streams between our fingers.
Time pretends to be generous,
Just like me, teaching the way within my ample belly,
Like the storms in legend,
The crowd waits, but it once again fails to show up,
Just like a person's lingering illness, never spoken of.

    September 26, 2025

蜉蝣生物

弦月是一隻羊角
掛著一片黑雲的布衫
大地失去了重心
樹影和樓群是一對連襟兄弟
還有那些趨炎附勢之徒
他們趁火打劫
密謀著一個歷史性的事件
竹子和木頭們，從夜色中浮上來
帶著秋蟲的低吟

和生死闊契的秘密
只有最深黑的重，才能在沉底之後
輕如鴻雁。才能
從肉身的臃腫裡，抽身而出

2025 年 9 月 27 日

Ephemeral Creatures

The crescent moon is a ram's horn,
Hanging from a black cloud's cloak.
The earth has lost its center,
The tree shadows and the buildings are like two close-knit brothers.
And there are those who court favor with power,
Taking advantage of the fire,
Plotting a historic event.
The bamboo and wood rise from the night,
Carrying the low hum of autumn insects

And the secret deals of life and death.
Only the deepest black weight, after sinking,
Can become as light as a wild goose. Only then,
Can one escape from the bloated heaviness of the body.

    September 27, 2025

杭州媽媽[1]

這是一條無限延長的線
到天盡頭,到黑盡的凌晨
你是那條線上
慣性滾動的輪子
具有衝破一切的勇氣
包括自己的耐力與身體的極限
凌晨四點,準備早餐
八點,送孩子,上班
下班,接孩子
工單,作業,菜市,廚房
這個無盡的閉環裡,沒有缺口
如今,在孩子們的天空裡
你成了那個
永遠補不上的巨大缺口

2025 年 9 月 29 日

[1].九月下旬 30 多歲的杭州媽媽凌晨四點起來為兩個孩子煮早餐,因長期勞累過度而猝死。

Hangzhou Mom

This is a line that stretches infinitely,
To the end of the sky, to the blackest of early mornings.
You are the wheel,
Rolling on that line by inertia,
With the courage to break through everything,
Including your own endurance and the limits of your body.
At four in the morning, preparing breakfast,
At eight, sending the children, then going to work,
After work, picking up the children,
Work orders, assignments, the market, the kitchen,
In this endless closed loop, there are no gaps.
Now, in the sky of your children,
You have become that
Enormous gap that can never be filled.

September 29, 2025

Note: A mother from Hangzhou in her 30s passed away suddenly after years of overwork. She woke up at 4 AM every day to prepare breakfast for her two children. She collapsed and died from exhaustion.

前 夜

鍋蓋鐵著一張黑臉
覆在青嶺山和冒火山之間。正如
一個口含著果核之人
說出的方言，含混不清

風猶疑不定
夜色是一張狗皮膏藥
今天貼在昨天的傷疤上
明天，又將覆滿今天的舊傷

兔子們咬緊牙關
貓頭鷹把眼睛藏在腋下
我卻看見它收斂的光芒
像一枚火種

2025 年 9 月 30 日

The Night Before

The lid of the pot presses down on a black face,
Covering the space between Qingling Mountain and the erupting volcano. Just as
A person with a fruit pit in their mouth
Speaks in a dialect, muffled and unclear.

The wind hesitates,
The night is like a dogskin plaster,
Today, it sticks to yesterday's scar,
Tomorrow, it will cover today's old wounds.

The rabbits clench their teeth,
The owl hides its eyes under its wing,
But I see its collected light,
Like a spark.

  September 30, 2025

评论

BOOK REVIEW

在構建與創新中表現思想的深度

——試論何中俊詩集《半寸山河》的藝術性與思想性

野 松

認識詩人何中俊,應該有近20年時間了。近年,因同在一個詩歌群,詩歌寫作的交流就更多了,他幾乎每天都將他寫的一首新作發給我。作為"每日一詩"詩歌運動的發起者,這麼多年來,他堅持每日寫一首詩,這種執著、堅韌,以及取得的成績,是讓我十分敬重的。堅持每日寫一首詩,是能讓自己的心靈保持著對這個世界這個人間的敏感度與激情的。而這部《半寸山河》,作為詩人何中俊2016年至2025年的詩歌精選集,所選作品雖不及其10年來所創作作品總量的十分之一,卻以其宏大的時間跨度與深邃的精神探索,構築了一座獨具個性的詩歌王國。從藝術性與思想性兩方面審視,這部詩集既體現了詩人對現代漢語詩歌技藝的持續錘煉,也深刻折射出其對個體生命、社會現實和存在本質的持續深入思考。

通過認真閱讀這部《半寸山河》詩集,我們可以發現,詩人何中俊的詩歌寫作具有鮮明的藝術個性特徵。

一是注重意象系統的構建與創新,其意象體系豐富而獨特。他善於將自然物象(如石頭、河流、月光、種子等)與人類境遇相互映照,並賦予其深刻的象徵意義。例如,"種子是大地的飛鳥",將生命的希望與追求的渴望詩性地結合,意象營造得十分奇特精妙。而這,乃源于詩人詩思之獨特,唯詩思之獨特才會帶來意象之新穎與奇特精妙。種子,本來是種於泥土裡的,但卻成了"大地的飛鳥",蓋因"種子"有理想,有信念之根,而具有了這些,必能長出翅膀,成為在大地之上飛翔的鳥。如"落在阿爾卑斯山的雪",則以雪的堅硬喻指不可磨滅的歲月故事與歷史遺存。這些意象既有傳統詩歌的意蘊,又融入了現代隱喻,使詩歌在視覺與意象層面具有多層次的美感。

二是注重語言的凝練與內斂，常通過具體詞彙、簡潔句式、富有張力的詞義組合，創造出內涵豐富的詩行。在《句子》一詩中，詩人將詩句比作"泥巴捏的"，在爐火中找回自己的身份；《詞語的閃電》中，"詞語終於回到故鄉""只有時間，劃開傷口/剩下的歲月，都是劫後餘生/閃電來臨，所有倒伏的/青草和蕨類，都挺直了腰身"，則展示了語言的再生能力。這種語言處理方式增強了詩歌的思辨性和藝術感染力，讓語言的密度與質感都得到有效的呈現。

三是注重在結構方面進行有益的探索。這部詩集以短詩為主，也有組詩。在結構上，詩人常通過重複、對照、遞進等手法強化詩意，如《悲憫之湖》中的"劍就懸在頭頂"與"愛的船舶，就會擱淺"形成對比。特別是二元對立審美情趣所營造出來的詩美，頗具張力，如"內心的火焰，是一首/慢慢涼下來的詩篇"（《寄身一滴春雨》）；"深度意象的詩人們在海底/看見天空的鳥兒展開了翅膀"（《深度意象》）；"靠在黃桷樹上的時候/我的身體就長出無數的根來/它們要回到大地上，就像我/總是要飛回天空裡"（《風口》）。組詩的結構也常見，如《南粵植物志系列之：荔枝/龍眼》《尋找博爾赫斯》《大雨，過白衣古寺》等，展現了詩人詩意表達的多面性與詩意建構的多重性。

四是注重現代主義與本土元素的詩性融合。何中俊的詩歌寫作深受西方現代詩人（如羅伯特·布萊、卡夫卡、博爾赫斯、卡爾維諾等）的影響，但他始終堅持本土立場。他對山川河海、歷史人物的詩意重構，體現了對中華文明的深厚情感。詩中既有對個體生命的體驗，如"父親的一生，就是彎腰/慢慢地長成一棵莊稼/造機器的張大勇，最後讓自己/成了零件，裝在一部大機器上"（《方式》），也有對宏大歷史的反思，如"你就是那一粒米/喂飽一個王朝的饑腸/長大了的人，才能與一個時代/同興衰，共短長"（《山陽道·魏風之王戎》），形成了獨特的藝術張力。

五是注重語言節奏與韻律的互應。詩集中的大部分詩作，節奏舒緩有致，韻律變化多樣，既有自由詩的奔放，也有內在韻律的克制。如《自由境界》中對小葉欖仁的描繪，展現了詩歌節奏與自然節奏的互應。

通過認真閱讀這部《半寸山河》詩集，我們可以發現，詩人在這些詩作裡所表現的思想內核深刻而又多層次。

一是對個體生命的體悟與個體尊嚴的演繹。詩集中反復探討個人在時代洪流中的位置。《在一朵薔薇裡看見自己的肉身》《我是這樣的一棵樹》《拙夫》等詩作，展現了詩人對自我價值和社會角色的思考。在《我們這些鳥蛋，孵在這蒼茫的人世》《一枚柿子》中對現代人的生活狀態和情感寄託提出追問。

二是對歷史與現實的批判性審視。如《秋後算帳》《歷史事件》《君子國》等作品，展現了對歷史事件、社會現象的反思。詩人對現代社會中人的異化、價值的失落發出詰問。例如，"在濕地公園"中對身份迷失的描繪，"挖地瓜"中對新舊交替的反思。

三是對自然與人文的和諧追求。詩集中，自然物象不僅是描摹對象，更是詩意的棲息地。如《春天這個皮匠》《萬物生》等詩表現了人與自然的和諧關係。

四是對存在主義的追問。詩集中的許多詩作，常從日常物象中透視生命本質，展現對存在意義的追問。如《縱虎者》《被掩埋的巨人》《困在語言的繭房》，體現了詩人對語言，對存在關係的深刻思考。

五是對詩意棲居的追求。詩集中的"山河"既是家國山河的映照，也是個體心靈空間的象徵。詩人以心靈為基，以語言為石，以微顯著，構建個體的"詩歌帝國"。在《自序》中，詩人以長城、金字塔、歌德《浮士德》和《四庫全書》為例，強調通過微小積累成就宏大事業的藝術追求。

作為詩人 10 年詩歌寫作的精選集，可以說，這部詩集裡有許多在藝術性與思想性高度融合，值得人們認真品讀與欣賞的作品。

如《失獨者在病房吞食往事的藥片》，就對親情，對生命，作了深刻的詩性揭示：

> 燈光昏暗不明，她的側身
> 像一隻荒原上失群的夜鶯
> 蹲在床頭。四周的靜
> 比水還冷漠。親人
> 都從背景裡漸漸退去

> 這骨髓裡長出來的疼痛
> 無法喊出。護士站
> 只是一個臨時的站台
> 每一個人到站以後
> 只能蘸著夜色的墨汁
> 和著往事的藥片，獨自吞咽
> 那一刻，我看見她的喉結
> 像一個巨大的山洞
> 她是自己脫下的一枚蟬蛻
> 獨自掛在無邊的夜色裡

　　現代詩歌的使命之一，是對主客觀世界進行形象化也即詩性的揭示。這首詩作對親情的揭示，從"在場"到"缺席"，讓人讀後有種被錐心刺肺的痛感。詩中的"親人/都從背景裡漸漸退去"，以具象的"退去"動作，揭示了親情在生命絕境中的脆弱性。這種"退去"並非物理空間的疏離，而是情感紐帶的斷裂——當命運將人拋入深淵，血緣關係反而成為映照孤獨的鏡子。詩人以"骨髓裡長出來的疼痛"，隱喻失獨者與逝去子女的共生關係，這種疼痛無法通過親情來撫慰，只能轉化為"獨自吞咽"的沉默與苦楚。護士站作為"臨時的站台"，進一步強化了親情的臨時性，暗示在生命終點，親情不過是匆匆過客，最終留下的仍是個體與死亡的直面。

　　這首詩作對生命的揭示，詩性地表現了在"蟬蛻"與"夜鶯"間的存在困境。詩中的"夜鶯"與"蟬蛻"構成雙重意象，分別指向生命的脆弱與蛻變。夜鶯在荒原失群，象徵人類在命運面前的渺小與無助；而蟬蛻的"獨自懸掛"，則揭示生命在失去延續性後的空洞。這種蛻變並非昇華，而是被剝離後的虛無，正如"喉結像巨大的山洞"，吞噬著往事的藥片卻無法消化。詩人通過"夜色的墨汁"這一意象，將生命置於永恆的黑暗中，暗示個體在時間洪流中的無力感——每一片往事藥片，都是對存在意義的質疑。

　　這首詩作的藝術手法十分精妙，其以物喻情的張力強勁。一是意象營造的陌生化,將"喉結"比作"山洞",突破生理特徵的常規表達,賦予其吞噬記憶的隱喻,強化了痛苦的內化過程。二是色彩呈現的冷峻,以"燈光昏暗不明""夜色的墨汁"構建壓抑的視覺空間,與"骨髓疼痛"的觸覺形成通感,營造出窒息般的氛圍。三是結構的留白,全詩未直接描寫失獨者的面容或情緒,僅通過"側身""蹲"等動作,讓讀者在沉默中感知其精神世界的崩塌。

儘管這首詩作以孤獨與死亡為主題,但"吞食往事藥片"的行為本身,已暗含對生命尊嚴的堅守。這種堅守並非對抗命運,而是在接受中完成自我救贖。正如詩人通過"夜色"的永恆性,將個體的悲劇昇華為人類共通的生存困境——我們都在吞咽往事的藥片,試圖在黑暗中尋找一絲光亮。此詩以極簡的語言,完成了對親情與生命的雙重解構。它不提供安慰,卻以藝術的力量讓讀者直面生命的荒誕與堅韌。在這首詩裡,每一個"獨自吞咽"的瞬間,都是對存在最深刻的叩問,對個體生命最真誠的悲憫。

如《瘦金體》一詩,通過書法藝術這一載體,將形式美感、歷史隱喻與精神氣節熔鑄為一體,展現出深厚的藝術張力與思想深度:

> 你真是瘦呀
> 我擔心你咳一聲
> 會咯出一口北宋的血來
> 因為瘦
> 才有自己的硬度
> 從你的身上
> 我看到文天祥
> 和袁崇煥骨頭裡合金的份量
> 瘦,不是家國病
> 是一種壓縮
> 是把胸中的萬里河山,壓縮成
> 一根竹竿的銀鉤鐵劃

此詩在藝術性方面,注重意象的淬煉與語言的雕塑。詩人以"瘦金體"為原點,構建了多重意象的關聯:"瘦"既是書法筆劃的視覺特徵,又通過"咳血"的擬人化瞬間勾連歷史創傷("北宋的血")。這種跳躍並非斷裂,而是以"瘦—硬—骨"為邏輯鏈,將書法、人體、歷史人物(文天祥、袁崇煥)自然串聯,形成意象的同心圓輻射,讓意象的跳躍與黏合得以完美的體現。而"骨頭裡合金的份量"將抽象的精神氣節轉化為可稱量的物理屬性,金屬質感呼應了"銀鉤鐵劃"的書法術語,同時暗含歷史苦難對人格的鍛造。而"壓縮"一詞更顯精妙——它既是書法中筆墨的凝練,也是山河氣韻在方寸間的精神提純,語言本身如瘦金體般"瘦而凝勁"。這種隱喻的縱深與質感讓該詩詩質上乘。此外,節奏與張力控制得十分精準。詩句長短錯落,從"咯出一口北宋的血來"的戲劇性爆發,到"胸中的萬里河山"的浩瀚鋪陳,最終收束於"一根竹竿的銀鉤鐵劃",形成張弛有度的呼吸感。這種節奏模擬了書法運筆的提按頓挫,詩形即筆意。

　　此詩在思想性方面,注重讓歷史重詮與精神立骨有效粘連起來。如對"瘦"的價值重估十分精準。詩人敏銳地剝離了"瘦"與"病"的慣性關聯("瘦,不是家國病"),將其重構為一種精神密度:"壓縮"不是衰微,而是將山河氣韻、歷史責任內化為個人風骨。這既是對瘦金體美學內核的解讀,亦是對中華民族危難中精神不折的隱喻。對歷史人格的符號焊接十分到位,文天祥(南宋)、袁崇煥(明)與北宋的瘦金體並置,打破了線性時間。詩人並非在考據歷史,而是在建構一種超越時代的精神譜系:不同時代的悲劇英雄通過"骨頭的合金"在文化符號中重逢,凸顯苦難中淬煉的民族脊樑。此外,還做到藝術與氣節的互文。瘦金體作為宋徽宗的藝術創造,其命運與北宋的衰亡緊密相連。詩人卻通過"壓縮"的辯證,將這一常被詬病為"柔弱"的藝術形式,轉化為精神硬度的象徵——藝術不僅是美的載體,更是苦難歷史的承受者與轉化者,在斷裂處生出堅韌。

　　這首詩的獨特價值在於,它並未停留在對瘦金體形式美的讚歎,也不止於懷古傷今。詩人以"瘦"為手術刀,剖開歷史表層,顯露出文化基因中那些被壓縮卻從未消散的精神能量。書法筆劃與民族脊樑在"硬度"上達成同構,個體命運與萬里河山在"壓縮"中實現共振。

最終，銀鉤鐵劃不僅是墨蹟，更是刻在歷史骨骼上的銘文。而詩的完成，本身即是對那種"壓縮"精神的釋放與舒展——仿佛一根竹竿在紙上生長出無形的山林，在當代重新呼吸。

文學作品只有表達出深意，才具有其存在的價值。詩歌作為一種十分注重語言藝術的文體，能表現出深刻的思想意蘊，已經算是比較成功的了。"半寸山河現彩霞。"何中俊的這部《半寸山河》詩歌精選集，堅守詩的抒情本質，在構建與創新中表現思想的深度，為現代漢語詩歌增添了沉實的一筆。詩集中構建的"詩歌帝國"，不僅是個體精神的棲居地，也是對個體生命尊嚴的堅守和對社會現實的敏銳批判。這"半寸山河"，雖微末卻深邃，是詩人精神家園的縮影，也是我們這個時代精神的見證。

詩歌寫作有了一定數量之後，就應向更高質量方面進展。我曾對何中俊建議過，每日一詩堅持到現在，不如每兩日一詩，或無需每日一詩，只需有靈感了才寫，而每寫一詩，都應做到極盡想像之力、思想之力、修辭之力，將之寫到最好。如今，面對這部詩歌精選集，我不知我的這個建議是對還是錯。但無論怎樣，我還是十分樂見何中俊的詩歌寫作成績的，對他對詩歌信念的堅執還是十分欣賞的。

2026.01.05

※野松，中國作家協會會員，中國文藝評論家協會會員，中國詩歌學會會員，廣東省作協詩歌委員會委員。

"A Rosy Cloud over Half an Inch of Rivers and Mountains":
Expressing Profound Ideology through Construction and Innovation
—On the Artistry and Ideological Depth of He Zhongjun's Poetry Collection Half an Inch of Rivers and Mountains

Ye Song

I have known the poet He Zhongjun for nearly twenty years. In recent years, as we are both members of the same poetry group, we have had more exchanges about poetry writing. He sends me almost one new poem he has written every day. As the initiator of the "One Poem a Day" poetry movement, he has persisted in writing one poem each day for all these years. His dedication, perseverance, and the achievements he has made command my great respect. Writing a poem every day enables one to keep one's soul sensitive and passionate about the world and human life. Half an Inch of Rivers and Mountains, a selection of He Zhongjun's poems written from 2016 to 2025, includes less than one-tenth of the works he has created over the decade. Nevertheless, with its grand time span and profound spiritual exploration, it constructs a distinctive poetic kingdom. From the perspectives of artistry and ideological depth, this collection not only reflects the poet's consistent refinement of modern Chinese poetic techniques but also profoundly mirrors his sustained and in-depth contemplation on individual life, social reality, and the essence of existence.

Through careful reading of Half an Inch of Rivers and Mountains, we can discern that He Zhongjun's poetry writing boasts distinct artistic characteristics.

First, it emphasizes the construction and innovation of an imagery system, which is rich and unique. He excels at juxtaposing natural objects (such as stones, rivers, moonlight, seeds, etc.) with human predicaments, endowing them with profound symbolic significance. For instance, the line "A seed is the bird of the earth" poetically combines the hope of life with the yearning for pursuit, creating an extraordinarily ingenious image. This originality stems from the poet's unique poetic thinking—only such thinking can give birth to novel and exquisite imagery. A seed, originally sown in the soil, becomes "the bird of the earth" because it harbors ideals and takes root in faith; with these, it is bound to grow wings and soar above the land. Another example is "The snow falling on the Alps", which uses the hardness of snow to symbolize the indelible stories of years and historical relics. These images not only retain the implications of traditional poetry but also incorporate modern metaphors, lending the poems multi-layered aesthetic appeal both visually and imaginatively.

Second, it stresses the conciseness and restraint of language. The poet often creates meaningful lines through specific vocabulary, succinct sentence structures, and tension-laden combinations of word meanings. In the poem Sentences, he compares verses to "things molded from mud" that reclaim their identity in the furnace fire. In The Lightning of Words, lines like "Words finally return to their hometown", "Only time slashes open the wound / The remaining years are all days after the catastrophe / When lightning strikes, all the prostrate / Grasses and ferns straighten their backs" demonstrate the regenerative power of language. This linguistic approach enhances the philosophical depth and artistic appeal of the poems, effectively presenting the density and texture of language.

Third, it engages in fruitful explorations of poetic structure. The collection mainly consists of short poems, along with some poem sequences. In terms of structure, the poet frequently employs techniques such as repetition, contrast, and progression to strengthen poetic meaning. For example, in The Lake of Compassion, the lines "The sword hangs overhead" and "The ship of love will run aground" form a striking contrast. Particularly, the poetic beauty generated by the aesthetic taste of binary opposition is full of tension, as seen in lines like "The flame within is a poem / Slowly cooling down" (Dwelling in a Drop of Spring Rain), "Poets of profound imagery see, at the bottom of the sea / Birds in the sky spreading their wings" (Profound Imagery), and "When I lean against the banyan tree / Countless roots grow out of my body / They want to return to the earth, just as I / Always want to fly back to the sky" (Windward). Poem sequences are also common, such as Series of Flora in Southern Guangdong: Litchi/Longan, In Search of Borges, and Heavy Rain Passing White Robe Ancient Temple, showcasing the poet's versatility in poetic expression and the multiplicity of poetic construction.

Fourth, it pursues the poetic integration of modernism and local elements. He Zhongjun's poetry writing is deeply influenced by Western modernist poets (such as Robert Bly, Franz Kafka, Jorge Luis Borges, Italo Calvino, etc.), yet he always adheres to a localized stance. His poetic reconstruction of mountains, rivers, seas, and historical figures reflects his profound affection for Chinese civilization. His poems encompass both reflections on individual life, as in "My father's life is a lifetime of bending over / Gradually growing into a crop / Zhang Dayong, who built machines, ended up turning himself / Into a part, installed on a great machine" (Ways), and meditations on grand historical themes, as in "You are that single grain of rice / Feeding the hunger of a dynasty / Only those who have matured can stand with an era / Sharing its prosperity and decline, its length and brevity" (Shanyang Road • Wang Rong in the Air of Wei), thus forming a unique artistic tension.

Fifth, it highlights the interplay between linguistic rhythm and rhyme. Most poems in the collection feature a moderate and well-paced rhythm with varied rhymes, embodying both the unrestrained vigor of free verse and the restraint of inherent musicality. For example, the depiction of the terminalia mantaly in The Realm of Freedom demonstrates the harmonious correspondence between poetic rhythm and the rhythm of nature.

A careful reading of Half an Inch of Rivers and Mountains also reveals that the ideological core embodied in these poems is profound and multi-layered.

First, it involves the comprehension of individual life and the interpretation of individual dignity. The collection repeatedly explores the position of the individual amid the torrent of the times. Poems such as Seeing My Own Flesh in a Rose, I Am Such a Tree, and The Clumsy Man reflect the poet's reflections on self-worth and social roles. Works like We Are These Bird Eggs, Incubating in This Vast World and A Persimmon pose inquiries into the living conditions and emotional sustenance of modern people.

Second, it carries out a critical examination of history and reality. Poems such as Settling Accounts After the Autumn Harvest, Historical Events, and The Land of Gentlemen showcase reflections on historical incidents and social phenomena. The poet raises questions about the alienation of humans and the loss of values in modern society. Examples include the portrayal of identity confusion in In the Wetland Park and the meditation on the transition between the old and the new in Digging Sweet Potatoes.

Third, it embodies the pursuit of harmony between nature and humanity. In the collection, natural objects are not merely subjects of description but also poetic habitats. Poems like Spring the Cobbler and All Things Grow express the harmonious relationship between humans and nature.

Fourth, it contains existential inquiries. Many poems in the collection penetrate the essence of life through everyday objects, revealing reflections on the meaning of existence. Works such as The Tiger-Releaser, The Buried Giant, and Trapped in the Cocoon of Language reflect the poet's profound contemplation on language and the relationship of existence.

Fifth, it represents the pursuit of poetic dwelling. The "rivers and mountains" in the collection are both a reflection of the nation's land and a symbol of the individual's spiritual space. Based on his soul, using language as stones, and revealing the profound through the trivial, the poet constructs his own individual "poetic empire". In the Preface, the poet cites examples such as the Great Wall, the Pyramids, Johann Wolfgang von Goethe's Faust, and The Complete Library of the Four Treasuries to emphasize his artistic pursuit of achieving grand undertakings through incremental accumulation.

As a selection of the poet's ten years of poetic creation, this collection undoubtedly contains many works that achieve a high integration of artistry and ideological depth, worthy of careful reading and appreciation.

Take A Parent Who Lost Their Only Child Swallows Tablets of the Past in the Ward for example, which offers a profound poetic revelation of family love and life:

> The light is dim and unclear, her side profile
> Like a nightingale lost from its flock on the wilderness
> Huddled by the bed. The silence all around
> Is colder than water. Relatives
> Gradually fade away from the background
> This pain that grows from the marrow

Cannot be cried out. The nurses' station
Is but a temporary platform
After everyone arrives at the station
They can only dip into the ink of the night
Mix it with the tablets of the past, and swallow alone
At that moment, I saw her Adam's apple
Like a vast cave
She is a cicada slough she shed herself
Hanging alone in the boundless night

One of the missions of modern poetry is to offer a vivid, that is, poetic, revelation of the subjective and objective worlds. This poem's revelation of family love, from "presence" to "absence", leaves readers with a piercing sense of sorrow. The line "Relatives / Gradually fade away from the background" uses the concrete action of "fading away" to reveal the fragility of family love in the face of life's desperate situations. This "fading away" is not physical distance but a rupture of emotional bonds—when fate hurls a person into the abyss, blood ties instead become a mirror reflecting loneliness. The poet uses the metaphor of "pain that grows from the marrow" to illustrate the symbiotic relationship between the bereaved parent and the deceased child. This pain cannot be soothed by family love; it can only be transformed into the silence and grief of "swallowing alone". The nurses' station, described as a "temporary platform", further emphasizes the temporariness of family love, implying that at the end of life, family love is merely a passing traveler, leaving the individual to confront death alone in the end.

In revealing the essence of life, the poem poetically depicts the existential predicament between "cicada slough" and "nightingale". The dual imagery of "nightingale" and "cicada slough" in the poem points to the fragility and transformation of life respectively. The nightingale lost on the wilderness symbolizes the insignificance and helplessness of humans in the face of fate; the "cicada slough hanging alone" reveals the emptiness of life after losing its continuity. This transformation is not a sublimation but a void left by being stripped away, just as "the Adam's apple is like a vast cave", swallowing the tablets of the past yet unable to digest them. Through the imagery of "the ink of the night", the poet places life in eternal darkness, implying the individual's sense of powerlessness amid the torrent of time—each tablet of the past is a question mark over the meaning of existence.

The artistic techniques employed in this poem are exquisite, with powerful tension in its use of objects to convey emotions. First, the defamiliarization of imagery: comparing the "Adam's apple" to a "cave" breaks away from conventional physiological descriptions, endowing it with the metaphor of devouring memories and intensifying the internalization process of pain. Second, the bleakness of color presentation: the dim light and "ink of the night" construct an oppressive visual space, which forms a synaesthesia with the tactile sensation of "marrow-deep pain", creating a suffocating atmosphere. Third, the structural blankness: the poem does not directly describe the bereaved parent's facial features or emotions, but only uses actions such as "side profile" and "huddled" to allow readers to perceive the collapse of their spiritual world in silence.

Although the poem takes loneliness and death as its themes, the act of "swallowing tablets of the past" itself implies a perseverance in the dignity of life. This perseverance is not a confrontation with fate but a form of self-redemption through acceptance. Just as the poet uses the eternity of "the night" to elevate the individual tragedy to a universal existential predicament—we all swallow tablets of the past, trying to find a glimmer of light in the darkness. With its minimalistic language, this poem achieves a dual deconstruction of family love and life. It offers no consolation, yet with its artistic power, it compels readers to confront the absurdity and resilience of life. In this poem, every moment of "swallowing alone" is a profound inquiry into existence and a sincere compassion for individual life.

Another example is Slender Gold Calligraphy, which, through the medium of calligraphic art, integrates formal beauty, historical metaphor, and spiritual integrity into a cohesive whole, demonstrating profound artistic tension and ideological depth:

> *You are truly slender*
> *I fear that if you cough once*
> *You will split up a mouthful of Northern Song blood*
> *Because of your slenderness*

> *You possess your own hardness*
> *From you*
> *I see the weight of alloy*
> *In the bones of Wen Tianxiang and Yuan Chonghuan*
> *Slenderness is not a national ailment*
> *It is a compression*
> *It is compressing the boundless rivers and mountains in your chest*
> *Into the silver hooks and iron strokes of a bamboo slip*

In terms of artistry, this poem focuses on the refinement of imagery and the sculpting of language. Taking "Slender Gold Calligraphy" as the starting point, the poet constructs connections between multiple layers of imagery: "slenderness" is not only a visual feature of calligraphic strokes but also, through the personified image of "spitting up blood", instantly links to historical trauma ("Northern Song blood"). This leap is not disjointed; instead, with the logical chain of "slenderness—hardness—bones", it naturally connects calligraphy, the human body, and historical figures (Wen Tianxiang, Yuan Chonghuan), forming a concentric radiation of imagery that perfectly embodies the leap and cohesion of images. The line "the weight of alloy in the bones" transforms abstract spiritual integrity into a measurable physical attribute; the metallic texture echoes the calligraphic term "silver hooks and iron strokes" while implying the forging of character through historical hardships. The word "compression" is particularly ingenious—it refers not only to the condensation of brush and ink in calligraphy but also to the spiritual purification of the aura of rivers and mountains within a tiny space. The language itself is as "slender yet condensed and forceful" as Slender Gold Calligraphy. This profound and textured metaphor elevates the poem to a superior level of poetic quality. Furthermore, the rhythm and tension are precisely controlled. The lines vary in length, progressing from the dramatic outburst of "spit up a mouthful of Northern Song blood" to the grand narration of "the boundless rivers and mountains in your chest", and finally converging on "the silver hooks and iron strokes of a bamboo slip", creating a rhythmic ebb and flow. This rhythm mimics the rise and fall of the brush in calligraphy, making the form of the poem a reflection of the calligrapher's brushwork intent.

In terms of ideological depth, the poem effectively integrates the reinterpretation of history with the establishment of spiritual backbone. For one thing, it offers an accurate re-evaluation of the value of "slenderness". The poet astutely separates "slenderness" from its habitual association with "ailment" ("Slenderness is not a national ailment"), reconstructing it as a form of spiritual density: "compression" is not decline but the internalization of the aura of rivers and mountains and historical responsibility into personal moral integrity. This is not only an interpretation of the aesthetic core of Slender Gold Calligraphy but also a metaphor for the unyielding spirit of the Chinese nation amid hardships. For another, it achieves a seamless symbolic connection of historical personalities. Wen Tianxiang (Southern Song Dynasty) and Yuan Chonghuan (Ming Dynasty) are juxtaposed with Northern Song's Slender Gold Calligraphy, breaking the linearity of time. The poet is not engaged in historical textual research but constructing a spiritual genealogy that transcends eras: tragic heroes from different times reunite in cultural symbols through the "alloy in their bones", highlighting the backbone of the nation forged through suffering. Additionally, it realizes the intertextuality between art and moral integrity. As an artistic creation of Emperor Huizong of Song, Slender Gold Calligraphy is closely linked to the decline of the Northern Song Dynasty. Yet through the dialectic of "compression", the poet transforms this art form, often criticized as "fragile", into a symbol of spiritual fortitude—art is not merely a carrier of beauty but also a bearer and transformer of historical suffering, generating resilience amid fragmentation.

The unique value of this poem lies in the fact that it does not stop at admiring the formal beauty of Slender Gold Calligraphy, nor does it merely indulge in nostalgic lament for the past. Taking "slenderness" as a scalpel, the poet cuts through the surface of history, revealing the spiritual energy within the cultural genes that, though compressed, has never dissipated. Calligraphic strokes and the nation's backbone achieve isomorphism in terms of "hardness"; individual fate and the boundless rivers and mountains resonate in the process of "compression".

In the end, the silver hooks and iron strokes are not merely ink marks but inscriptions carved into the bones of history. And the completion of the poem itself is a release and expansion of that "compressed" spirit—as if a bamboo slip grows invisible mountains and forests on paper, breathing anew in the contemporary era.

A literary work only possesses value if it expresses profound meaning. As a genre that attaches great importance to linguistic art, poetry can be regarded as quite successful if it can convey profound ideological implications. "A rosy cloud over half an inch of rivers and mountains." He Zhongjun's poetry collection Half an Inch of Rivers and Mountains upholds the lyrical essence of poetry and expresses ideological depth through construction and innovation, making a solid contribution to modern Chinese poetry. The "poetic empire" constructed in the collection is not only a habitat for individual spirit but also a defense of individual life dignity and an acute critique of social reality. This "half an inch of rivers and mountains", though tiny, is profound—it is a microcosm of the poet's spiritual homeland and a testament to the spirit of our times.

After reaching a certain quantity in poetry writing, one should strive for higher quality. I once suggested to He Zhongjun that after persisting with "one poem a day" for so long, he might switch to writing one poem every two days, or even abandon the daily routine altogether, writing only when inspiration strikes. Whenever he writes a poem, he should exert his utmost imagination, ideological depth, and rhetorical skills to make it the best it can be. Now, facing this selected poetry collection, I am not sure whether my suggestion was correct. Nevertheless, I am very pleased to witness He Zhongjun's achievements in poetry writing and deeply admire his unwavering commitment to poetry.

January 5, 2026

※Ye Song is a member of the China Writers Association, the China Literature and Art Critics Association, the China Poetry Society, and a member of the Poetry Committee of the Guangdong Writers Association.

www.ingramcontent.com/pod-product-compliance
Lightning Source LLC
Chambersburg PA
CBHW060511080526
44586CB00012B/454